RON REYNOLDS

Also by Dave Bowler

Shanks, the Authorised Biography of Bill Shankly
No Surrender, a Biography of Ian Botham
Danny Blanchflower, a Biography of a Visionary
Winning Isn't Everything . . . a Biography of Alf Ramsey
Three Lions on the Shirt: Playing for England

RON REYNOLDS

The Life of a 1950s' Footballer

DAVE BOWLER AND
DAVID REYNOLDS

ORION

First published in Great Britain in 2003 by Orion
an imprint of Orion Books Ltd
Orion House, 5 Upper St Martin's Lane,
London WCH 9EA

A CIP catalogue record for this book is
available from the British Library

ISBN 0 75285 999 4

Printed and bound by Butler & Tanner Ltd,
Frome and London

CONTENTS

To Mom & Dad for everything; to Lisa for believing, and to Jonathan and Sophie – do your best and you will be the best. Thank you all for paying the price football still demands. D.B.

PREFACE

Football matches trigger a wealth of emotions and invariably pre-match pub discussions reveal common but abnormally encyclopaedic capabilities for remembering apparent historical trivia. A Chelsea-supporting business acquaintance has just informed me that Jimmy Greaves scored his first goal for the club against Spurs – you were in goal apparently. You never mentioned it and I was not aware.

Saturday 15 March 2003 and here I am, somewhat disinterested and certainly mute compared with my normal vocal involvement, sat at the Milton End, Fratton Park, at the invitation of a Wolves-supporting mate, watching Portsmouth v Wolverhampton Wanderers. Shades of often recalled pre-war encounters between two such famous teams. Poor game, well supported, in a ground that has not changed that dramatically for over forty years. The only difference is that I am wedged into a plastic bucket seat (at least some of the time) rather than standing on the terraces behind the goal, watching Shaka Hislop perform for Pompey rather than John Milkins. Paul Ince leads the visitors – in your day it would have been Billy Wright or Bill Slater. The ground is still bordered by terrace houses, the rickety fences and graffiti-covered walls, relics of old First Division battles in front of 40,000 swaying to and fro, with the same icy blast whipping off the Solent cutting through the gaps in the stands. How many of the 19,500 'sell out' crowd here today would have been present all those years ago for the local derby against Saints, when you, unknowingly, played your last game? I warrant a large proportion will recall the score and goalscorers, but would they remember you and your injury?

I cannot say that we were that close as father and son, for a variety of reasons. What did bring us together on a common platform was football – your career, and my interest, and although we were subsequently jointly responsible for running a successful business for in excess of twenty-five years, it was as business partners rather than relatives. I wonder how many discover unknown facets of a late parent's life after death, opening up all sorts of 'what if' 'why' 'how' and 'where' questions? Undoubtedly you were secretive in your private life, jealously ring-fencing us from the professional life, almost to the extent of treating the two as separate worlds. Mum preferred to remain outside, rarely being permitted entry into this closeted club, the dutiful wife bringing up a family and retaining the traditional role of housewife. One game early in your career at Aldershot was enough – witnessing you being carried off injured, led to an uttered 'never again' and that was how it stayed. Of all the family I was the only one allowed into your professional football career in the mid to late 1950s, even to the extent of being tolerated in the Spurs changing room prior to, at half time and at the end of a game and sitting in the dugout during the event. All of 7 years old, I was raised with the smell of liniment and the taste of half-time hot sweet tea. How was one so young expected to comprehend the machinations of a cold winter Saturday afternoon, whilst players sat listening to a ranting and raving boss (Rowe, Anderson, Nicholson), steam drifting from wet, muddy, sweaty bodies to congregate in a thick embrocation-induced blanket of cloud under the ceiling? The noise of the crowd still infiltrated into the bowels of the ground; deep underneath the stands, the tension was obvious. I listened and took it all in but said little. At the end of the game, all the players jumped into the same swilling, brown dirge they called a bath. Many would be smoking and I would go home wondering why my clothes permanently reeked of stale changing room. Some things do change, but invariably those images clearly remain in my head, evoking weird memories, particularly if I watch a game at White Hart Lane.

Stood shoulder to shoulder at the 1976 Saints v Man Utd Cup Final singing 'Abide with Me' was one of the very few occasions when we actually went to a match together. Your coaching and scouting activities immediately after retirement from football put paid to that, and then involvement in the business which took up at least part of each Saturday for both of us, restricted further opportunities. Working with each other during the week, socialising together at weekends did not appeal. The congregation sang the same anthem at your funeral service – it always has and always will bring a lump to my throat, and triggers off memories of the many occasions I sat on the touchline, or later on in the stands. I lost count of the number of times you were unable to finish a game through injury and I would be taken in hand by one or more of the team officials, and assisted to get back home whilst you languished in hospital. Goalkeepers just do not suffer injuries these days to the extent you did. You achieved a semi-final place but never got to Wembley – only now can I begin to appreciate your thoughts in 1976. You would never have voluntarily revealed them.

It was unnerving to say the least, rummaging around in drawers and cupboards after your death, discovering medals and trophies from around the world, many for the first time. The unknown quantity spilled from a bedroom storage cupboard – Mum was unaware (or perhaps disinterested) in the contents – 'Dad's football cuttings and such'. I sat for who knows how long, surrounded by an absolute wealth of brown-tinged, curled press cuttings, photographs, programmes, original letters, scrapbooks and meticulous accounts record books – a whole archived record dating back to the beginnings of your career, 1945 onwards. Spellbound, I read report after report of your performances – the words 'heroic' 'brave' 'England potential' 'carried off with concussion/head injury' continually springing from page after page. This was my dad they were talking about. Hundreds of programmes for matches against teams as diverse as Barnet to Blackpool, Man Utd to Boston Utd, and Kiev to Canada. You even participated in some of the first skirmishes with our Continental cousins in the forerunner of the UEFA Cup. Notwithstanding the memorabilia, rightly or wrongly, I could not help but ponder that the sum total of twenty years' effort, dedication, discipline and confrontation was a pair of shiny large Spurs shorts – I tried them on for size, elastic still holding firm, full and preliminary coaching badges, trophies green and bronzed with age. Your Acme Scoutmaster coaching whistle.

Your achievements were many in the face of adversity, you were undoubtedly ahead of your time in terms of tactics, player representation, man management, fitness and coaching acumen, but at the culmination of your time in football, the irony is that you had little to show for it. Your career was very much one of missed opportunities, unfortunate injuries and confrontation with influential personnel, many of whom you did not see eye to eye with. Your career suffered as a consequence of your principles, which never wavered.

My Father died on 2 June 1999 – his 71st birthday. His footballing exploits spanned the period from just after the Second World War until injury enforced retirement in the mid 1960s. Very few would have been aware of his penchant (obsession even), for record keeping, nor the volumes (two very large boxes) of documents squirreled away over a twenty-year career. It took me several months to catalogue the material but as I absorbed the historical importance (if only to the family) it gradually dawned on me that perhaps there was sufficient substance and interest for publication of a diary on the life of a goalkeeper before the lifting of the maximum wage – a 'then and now' scenario, a comparison between Reynolds and a modern contemporary – Seaman, David James or Barthez?

Great idea, but how would I, a layman in such matters, even start to approach such a mammoth task? 'There is a book in all of us' did not convince me that I too had the capability, notwithstanding the question of allocating adequate time to conduct such an exercise. I had recalled Dad meeting many sports journalists, several authors and sports writers in his time, and indeed had contributed to various newspaper articles, biographies of colleagues (Ramsey, Blanchflower, Ted Bates) and even participated in a weekly boys' comic football page. I needed a professional view, hence calls to authors who had previously interviewed Dad (his forthright views on the game, fellow players, managers and directors were a journalist's dream), in the hope that perhaps they would be able to recall suitable anecdotes and perchance retained records or even taped interviews. Was the diary a viable proposition?

Three years later with the co-operation of Ian Preece of Orion, much hard work, research, extreme patience and interviews by author Dave Bowler, and here we are.

Forthright with opinions, unflinching in principle, stubborn to the extent that change of mind was not an option, Ron Reynolds was respected right throughout professional football, from groundsmen to managers, referees, administrators (but perhaps not some of the early directors) and many, many players with whom he performed at Aldershot, Spurs and Southampton. This is not just a verbatim record of his career, but a valid historical comment on then and now. Could there be a greater contrast between 1945 – for his first game Dad supplied his own boots, shin pads, string goalkeeping gloves and jersey, was paid a pittance and had to find his own way to the ground – and the cosseted, mollycoddled existence of the modern keeper, albeit with different pressures from media and the like?

I hope you enjoy the book as much as I have enjoyed assisting with the compilation.

My thanks to my wife Susan for her patience, and to all the family for their input and indulgence. Likewise all of those who have made a contribution, especially old colleagues and school friends of Dad's, for recalling 'missing link' information.

David Reynolds

October 29—November 4, 1947   (Registered at the G.P.O. as a Newspaper.)

ALDERSHOT KEEPER IN FORM

REYNOLDS, Aldershot's young goalkeeper, gave a plucky display against Newport County on Saturday. He is seen punching clear over the shoulder of MOGFORD, County's centre forward. Aldershot left-back SHEPPARD runs in to cover.

INTRODUCTION

There are few examples of Brian Glanville's prodigious output on the beautiful game that don't refer to Helenio Herrera, *catenaccio*, Internazionale, or Italian football in some fashion, however tenuous the link. But, if you scour his literary canon diligently enough, you'll come across one phrase that has no Italian connection – unless it's some hidden paean to the wonders of Dino Zoff – but which is the cornerstone of this book.

'Goalkeepers', says Glanville, 'are different.' And the sage of Serie A is right. Goalkeepers *are* different. Very different. And among goalkeepers, Ron Reynolds was a little more different yet.

Unless you are of a certain age – over fifty, I'm afraid – a devotee of the football of the 1950s, or a historian of Tottenham Hotspur or Southampton, the name Ron Reynolds is likely to have passed you by. For, though Ron was a goalkeeper good enough to grace the top of the old First Division for several seasons, he's sadly typical of the breed. Unless they happen to be a rare superstar in the Yashin, Banks, Shilton or Schmeichel mould, goalkeepers end up being footnotes in football history. But Reynolds was a very fine English goalkeeper, who only just missed a place in England's squad for the 1958 World Cup. And he more than played his part in Tottenham's all-consuming drive towards the then-mythical League Championship and FA Cup Double, which the club finally achieved in 1960/61, the first to do so in modern times. A machine such as the one being built at White Hart Lane ate up and spat out a number of players in its relentless search for footballing perfection. It had to be a thoroughly ruthless, unsentimental set up, and Reynolds was one of the casualties along the way. But, like others who weren't there when the medals were finally collected in May 1961, he'd been a vital cog in the machine.

Ron was a product of pre-war Britain, a friend and tactical confidant of Spurs' captain and intellectual spark Danny Blanchflower, and one of the graduates of Walter Winterbottom's Lilleshall coaching school. He was a player of the pre-Best era, a man of rare moral rectitude, who believed in behaving in a fashion befitting a professional sportsman. More impressive yet, Reynolds took those beliefs into his life post-football when he carved out a successful career as a financial adviser, always supporting the underdog. In a financial world that has more than its fair share of sharks and hawks, Reynolds was one of the doves, though that didn't mean he was a pushover when it came to business. His determination to ensure that justice prevailed meant that he was wholly trustworthy and won plenty of battles on behalf of those for whom he fought. Sometimes, however, there was a price to be paid, as Ron's son, and business partner, David recalls: 'He was a great one for chasing lost causes. If somebody was wronged he'd pursue it, if only to get the satisfaction of winning. I used to think that was all very well and laudable, but it wasn't making any money for us!'

Those traits served him well as a man, but also cost him dear as a footballer. He was a great believer in the Players' Union and worked diligently to see it achieve its ends, a stance which inevitably put him at odds with employers. Bosses in the 1950s tended to view the relationship between themselves and their employees as little different to that between masters and serfs. These were the days of the maximum wage and the retention system of contracts, whereby no player could leave his club without their express say so. Yet the players frequently had no greater security than a one-year contract. To call it soccer slavery, as Jimmy Hill did in one of his more emotive outbursts, was perhaps a little strong, but the restraints placed on men who had often been fighting for a rather greater freedom against the most fearsome German outfit in history just a decade earlier was odious at best. Reynolds, as anyone who knew him would expect, could not help but speak out against the system, and he made his fair share of enemies in the corridors of power as a result. Did that cause him to lose out to Bill Brown as the last line of defence of Bill Nicholson's immortal side? Certainly he was a more expendable presence than his cohort and partner in crime, Blanch-flower. If they couldn't dump Danny, at least they could get rid of Ron.

In defence of those who took issue with him, Reynolds was an undeniably stubborn character. In that sense, of course, he was ideal goalkeeping material. Contrary to the popular myth, goalkeeping does not demand a degree of insanity, but rather a strong sense of purpose. The keeper is the beautiful game's passion killer, its most successful form of contraception, dedicated to preventing the foot-balling orgasm, the goal. He's football's spoilsport, the man who is out to ruin everything, to destroy creativity, to nullify moments of great artistry, to prevent a match reaching its full potential. He's the man who lives to hear the commentators intoning 'nil' when the scores are read out on a Saturday night, while all the rest of us are waiting for a rash of '5–4' scorelines.

ALDERSHOT

CHAPTER ONE

Early days training on Aldershot Rec.

'We went down to the Portsmouth–Southampton game at Fratton Park. I was at the match with friends. Dad took us down there in the car, because it was the big local game and we all wanted to see it and see him in goal for Southampton. I remember there was a corner or free-kick. Portsmouth all went up into the box but it was cleared pretty quickly and Saints were on the attack. All the players started tearing off down the other end of the field, but I looked back and saw the old man was really struggling. His shoulder was just ripped right out. You could see it sagging halfway down where his arm should be. It was horrible, absolutely horrible. I was just a kid stuck in the crowd, not knowing what to do. He got carted off to hospital, and I think it was the trainer, Jimmy Gallacher, who picked up me and my mates and took us down to the local hospital to see him. Then drove us and Dad home.'

David Reynolds on the injury that ended the career of his father Ron, goalkeeper with Aldershot, Tottenham Hotspur and Southampton. Initially, it seemed like just another, if slightly more serious injury in the ever-increasing catalogue that afflicted Ron and his goalkeeping brethren. This time, though, the injury would never heal correctly and that was that.

It was no great surprise that injury should have the final say, given that Reynolds plied his trade in a very different footballing era from today's, particularly for those in his position. Nowadays, goalkeepers are protected by a total exclusion zone that seems to extend as the seasons go by. Anyone having the temerity to jump anywhere near the keeper today is almost certain to concede a free-kick and receive the benefit of some refereeing wisdom into the bargain. When Ron sustained his final injury, less than forty years ago, it was at a time in the game when a goalkeeper wasn't sacrosanct. He was an Aunt Sally, there to be attacked by any passing forward who felt he might be able to barge the ball into the net.

Just a few years earlier, in 1957, Peter McParland had won the FA Cup for Aston Villa with an assault on Ray Wood that left Wood a passenger on the wing and Jackie Blanchflower forced to take over between the sticks. It was a perfectly legal challenge on the field of play; had it taken place on the high street, it would have been bordering on the GBH side of violent assault. But it was the kind of challenge you would see week in, week out, up and down the Football League. Goalkeepers were fair game, stuck in a job that should have come with an occupational injury policy.

Still, as it ended, so had it begun: the Reynolds career was topped and tailed by an odd symmetry, circumstances symptomatic of the way in which clubs treated their serf-like employees. Not long after Ron had started playing the professional game, he sustained his first serious injury. Nowadays, if a David Seaman or a Fabien Barthez were to pick up any kind of serious knock, he'd be straight off to the best local hospital, ferried home in a private ambulance and given the very best private care, followed by rehabilitation under expert eyes. For Ron, it was a little different . . .

The 1947/48 season began on 23 August at the tail end of one of the driest summers on record. Compton and Edrich were each racking up thousands of runs while the sun perpetually shone. In those days football enjoyed a reasonable close-season lull. This year there were mutterings of complaint because the players had been away for 'only' ten weeks – the shortest break on record at that point. Aldershot journeyed to the seaside to begin their Third Division South campaign, and, as the local press reported, 'On the bone-hard grounds, injuries were inevitable.' In temperatures that topped 80°F, 'Reynolds, in a daring effort to prevent a goal, collided with Shaw, Torquay's inside-right, and both men were knocked out. Shaw recovered after the game had been held up for five minutes, but Reynolds was taken to hospital suffering from a suspected fractured skull. Sears deputised for the remainder of the game. Medical examination, however, revealed a lacerated scalp which needed two stitches.' The injury could have been far worse, but as it was, it meant that Ron had to spend a few hours in the local casualty department. While he was having his head stitched, his colleagues were setting off for home, leaving the young keeper stranded in Torquay, and having to make his own way home. What better demonstration could a young pro have of football's indifference to its employees? And these were the clubs who complained if a player wanted to move on, criticising their lack of loyalty!

It was a lesson reinforced five days later when Ron received the letter reproduced overleaf from the club chairman.

For all that Aldershot's treatment of their players left a great deal to be desired, the struggling club would ultimately prove to be Reynolds' gateway to a career with Tottenham and Southampton. On the surface, his seemed a fairly placid life, always living in and around the A3 corridor, in deepest Surrey and Hampshire, from Haslemere to Portsmouth and back again. Yet this apparently normal, suburban life belies an enigmatic and mysterious family background, as Ron's son David explains. 'He was born and brought up in Haslemere, but there's still this unknown factor of where the family originally came from. My grandfather wanted to go and visit my aunt in Australia a few years back, so he had to apply for a passport, and there was a lot of trouble finding all the right documentation, especially his birth certificate – nobody could track it down.

'Then they found somewhere along the line that when he was younger, somebody had changed his name from Jacobs to Reynolds – nobody knows why it was, but we've subsequently uncovered a Gran Jacobs further back down the family. That was why they

ALDERSHOT FOOTBALL CLUB LTD.

TELEGRAPHIC ADDRESS:
FOOTBALL, ALDERSHOT
TELEPHONE: ALDERSHOT 11

SECRETARY/MANAGER
W. McCRACKEN

RECREATION GROUND.
ALDERSHOT.

27th August 1947.

My Dear Reynolds,

 No doubt you have imagined that we had forgotten you. Let me say right away that you have continually been in our thoughts and wondered how you were getting on after that 'bump' last Saturday. We have phoned the Office on two occasions to make enquires, in the hope that you might have been at work, but of course drew a blank each time.

 As you might imagine, we have had many enquiries about you. One gentleman from Plymouth even rang up to know how you were. We could not tell him much, except to say that you managed to reach home safe and we hope sound.

 I am voicing the expression of the whole of the Club Directors and Players alike, when I sincerely trust that you will soon be about and whats more in harness once more. If you can manage it we should be happy to hear from you to know how you are progressing, and whether you have any ill effects after the accident.

 If Mr. McCracken approves, I may come over to see you sometime tomorrow Thursday, and if I can persuade him, he may come also

 In the meantime, take things easy, and the very best of good wishes for a speedy recovery from us all.

Yours Sincerely,

W.J. Strohal

Kind regards to your Father.

couldn't track down the birth certificate for the passport. When they finally knew where to look, the birth certificate was traced and he got his passport, but the poor old soul had a heart attack and passed away before he could go to Australia. Perhaps it was all the strain of trying to find the certificate.

'My grandfather had moved around a lot. When he was younger, he and his brother, who were living in Kingston-upon-Thames at the time, just suddenly put all their belongings up on to a horse and cart one day and shot down what is now the A3. They moved to the Hammer area, just a few miles from Haslemere.'

Whether the sudden flight and the name change are in any way connected is uncertain, though if the Jacobs brothers were fleeing from someone or something, the two probably went hand in hand, particularly as this was at a time when anti-Semitism was on the rise throughout Europe, including in the UK. In the political situation of the age clearly they felt it better to hide their Jewish origins and change the family name from Jacobs to Reynolds. It might not have been the reason for their flight, but for a pair seeking a fresh start, a clean break with everything from the past must have seemed seductive.

Once they'd traversed Surrey, the Reynolds family began to put down roots, and the upshot of the move was that young Ron benefited from a stable environment once he appeared on the scene on 2 June 1928. David Reynolds points out, 'Dad was born in Shottermill, then brought up in Lion Lane in Haslemere, where there was a whole congregation of Reynolds family and relatives: they had about half a dozen houses between them. The last remaining member of that family has just died and he was still in Lion Lane, so unfortunately it's the end of an era. Dad went to Shottermill School, and then on to Godalming County when he was older.'

Like most of his contemporaries growing up in the depression-ridden 1930s, life wasn't easy for the young Ron, especially in the light of tragic personal circumstances. His sister Gladys, or Bunt as she was better known, explains: 'My mother died when I was nine, Ron was six and Joan was only three. When she died, it was thought we'd all have to go in a home because Dad obviously had to work. But Gran Riddle's family lived next door and they said they'd look after us. Little Joan was brought up in their house and Ron and I stayed in our place next door. We were very close when we were young. We had a strict upbringing, which I'm sure made a mark on Ron because he was that way himself. I remember that Dad was very old fashioned. When I was sixteen, he would let me go out to a dance only if it was on a Saturday night – there was never any chance that he would let me go in the middle of the week. I remember one Saturday I was getting ready to go out and I'd put on red nail varnish. When we sat down to eat and he saw it, he got up from the table and said, "You take that off! I will not sit down at a table to eat with you while you have that on!" So I had to get up and take off my nail varnish, because he didn't like it.'

Perhaps the south was not as hard hit as the north and Scotland, regions savaged by the economic collapse that followed in the wake of the Wall Street Crash, but life in Surrey at that time was no picnic either. It's likely that most of Ron's values – his integrity, his belief in hard work as the route to success, his lifelong aversion to debt – were instilled in him by both the surrounding family and by his own experience, as Bunt suggests: 'We were both very self-sufficient from an early age because we had to be. But we never went hungry and even in the war we always did well. My gran couldn't read or write because she never went to school. The school she was supposed to go to was a long way to walk so she didn't go! But she was sharp, and her arithmetic was wonderful – I remember being in the butcher's once, wishing the ground would open up; I felt so awful because he'd charged a few pence too much! She knew exactly what she was due back when she won on the horses. Some of those bets were pretty complicated – doubles, trebles, yankees – but she could work out the odds.'

Ron clearly inherited that mathematical capacity, while simulta-neously assimilating the lesson that, in short, the key to life was putting food on the family table, a roof over their heads and clothes on their back. Nobody would do it for you, so you had to get out there, work hard and earn everything you wanted. That may sound like an almost monastic devotion to the virtues of hard work leading to an unremitting existence of grim toil and struggle, but that was far from the case. The Reynolds family was a happy one, with more than its fair share of characters, some of whom roped the young boy into their schemes. David Reynolds remembers his father telling him tales 'about his grandmother, who loved the horses and she was forever putting a few bob on the gee-gees, at a time when there were no betting shops or anything like that. So she used to get Dad to act as the bookies' runner. She'd give him the money, tell him which horse she wanted the money on, where and when it was running, and he'd run off to see the local chap who acted as the bookie. It must have had an effect on him. To my knowledge, until he put a few bob on the Lottery, he'd never had a bet, definitely never put any money on the football pools. He was very anti-betting generally, maybe because he saw his grandmother lose so much when he was younger. He thought it was a mug's game.'

Bunt confirms that view: 'When he was older, he was the part-owner of a greyhound with his uncle. After the dog had finished with racing, I think his uncle kept it as a pet. But I'm sure Ron never bet on it.

'Ron loved dogs when he was a boy. Our aunt had one called Toby and Ron used to cling to it. One day Ron had hold of it tight that the dog got frightened, lashed out and bit him across the mouth. Ron needed stictches.

'When he was just a toddler he got lost once, just wandered off. When we came to look for him, we found the dog had gone as well, so we knew that he'd be fine because the dog was with him. We found the pair of them in the woods.'

Pictures of the immediate pre- and post-war stock of young English footballers in the main reveal two types: the strapping young lad, six feet tall, built like a shed, who'd come to the game from a factory, a dockyard or a building site; and the whippet, the wiry lad who was pipe-cleaner thin and wouldn't recognise a steak if you put it over a black eye. Surprisingly for someone who ended up in the most physical of footballing roles, Ron fell into the latter category, possibly because his grandmother had worn him out, making him run to and from the bookies'. 'Dad was quite a skinny little thing,' says David. 'Even when he was fourteen or fifteen years old he wasn't tall in comparison with some of the boys competing against him in athletics competitions. In that way, he must have been a bit of a late developer.' Which would explain the length of time it took him to take up the goalkeeper's jersey, for his was no lifelong love affair with the number-one shirt. He saw himself as an outfielder as a boy; inevitable, perhaps, given his stature. These, after all, were the days of the nippy inside-forward, and it was as a goalscorer and creator that Ron initially cast himself. But as is so often the case with young goalkeepers, he ultimately went in goal not by choice, but through necessity: one day at school the team found itself short of a keeper. One impressive display later and the die was cast: Ron Reynolds' footballing days would be spent as the last line of defence. However, he still tried to fight the inevitable whenever possible: as a teenager in the ATC, he usually played in his preferred inside-forward position, only occasionally venturing as far back down the formation as wing-half.

John Brine was a contemporary of Ron's and recalls that, in the ATC, 'We played in the Guildford Pre-Service League, against army cadets and that sort of thing. I was a little older than Ron and the skipper of the side which won a couple of cups. He was quite a clever footballer. He wasn't a big lad at the time and he came in as other boys grew up and left. My brother was skipper before me and left to join the RAF, for instance, so there was a fair turnover of players.

'Back when we were kids things were a lot more cliquey, a lot more parochial, and although Haslemere, where I lived was only just up the road from Shottermill, people didn't really mix too much. You tended to stay where you were, you went to the village school. Now, of course, you have bigger schools and the kids mix from far and wide. We didn't do that, we were all very small groups of people.'

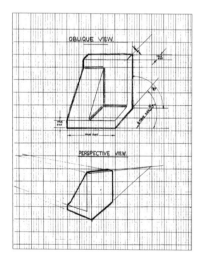

Ron's appreciation of angles picked up while at the Admiralty proved invaluable for his goalkeeping. This is a detail from his exercise book for a day-release course at the Government Training Centre, Hounslow, August 1944

Like the majority of his contemporaries, Ron never saw a career for himself in the game, especially as professional football was about to find itself on the back burner because of the war. Ron was just too young to be one of the unfortunates who ended up on a foreign field, however. What's more, his great talent in another area meant that he was destined for a reserved occupation, as David Reynolds explains: 'He used to love drawing, it was one of his great hobbies, and he was very, very good at it, both free-form drawing and as a technical artist, designing things. His dad had been a painter and decorator, so maybe it stemmed from that. After he left school, he started off as a draughtsman. The Admiralty had a place near where he lived, at Lythe Hill, and he worked there for a while before moving on to Dennis Brothers out in Guildford. Of course, they designed and built fire engines, so at the time that was all very important war work. There are still some of his old Dennis Brothers drawings around at home. He kept everything like that.'

Although he was now working, Ron continued to play local-league football at weekends. As conscientious towards his football as he was towards his profession, he continued to work on his all-round game in a position that he had arrived at late in the day. With the attention to detail that characterised all aspects of his life, he gradually worked on every area of his performance, identifying flaws and attempting to iron them out, as much for his own satisfaction as for improving the prospects of the team.

Though he might not have fully appreciated it at the time, Ron was preparing himself for a career in the family business, because playing football had been a tradition among his relatives. His grandfather, Alfie Riddle, a giant of a man, played for Small Heath FC before they turned professional and became Birmingham City. When Alfie moved south he was one of the founders of Shottermill FC, a team that boasted assorted members of the Riddle and Reynolds families for many years.

Ultimately, Ron's assiduous attention to his hobby was to pay healthy dividends. A career change was waiting just around the corner.

Shottermill Football Club, 1919-20.

A. F. Roe (Captain).　　A. G. Riddle (Hon. Sec).　　J. White (Vice-Captain).

C. Rapson　　E. Roe　　W. Balcomb　　A. Mullard　　P. Booker.　　T. J. Evans　　C. Snelling　　T. Rapson.
(Com.)　　(Trainer.)　　(Com.)　　　　　　　　　　　　　　　　　　　　　(Linesman.)　　(Com.)

L. E. Young.　　A. W. Partlett.　　H. M. Reynolds.　　W. A. Fenycate.　　H. F. Bargery.

14

CHAPTER TWO

There can't be too many footballers who have better documented their careers, certainly in its early stages, than Ron Reynolds. That was the legacy of his meticulous attention to detail, which served him so well in his pre-football career, and his interest in keeping immaculate records, which served him well after football, when he went into the financial services market.

As a result, on his death, he left behind a multitude of clippings, notebooks detailing his footballing income, photographs, booklets, programmes, tickets, a mass of memorabilia. The pick of the collection dates from Ron's time at Aldershot, and provides a fascinating snapshot of the ordinary footballer's way of life just after the war. Post-war Aldershot was about as unglamorous as the footballer's lot could get, bumping along in the Third Division South with promotion nowhere to be seen on the horizon.

Given Ron's brushes with the great and the good of the game, it was no surprise that he should be interviewed, his memories trawled through in connection with his time in football. I met him on several occasions, ostensibly to discuss the careers of Alf Ramsey and Danny Blanchflower, but conversations with Ron would always diverge from the intended path. Asked why he was such an inveterate chronicler of his career, his answer was: 'People weren't so blasé about joining a football club as they are now, which is odd, I suppose. Then, it wasn't a particularly well-paid job, it didn't put you on a different financial footing to most other people the way it does now, so you'd think people would be much more excited about the prospect today. I suppose we were more innocent or naïve in general in those days, and becoming involved with a football club just seemed such an unlikely or remarkable thing to do that I wanted to record it. I don't think I was alone in that. A lot of young players would have had scrapbooks kept by their parents or things like that. To be at a professional football club and then to play in the first team was almost unimaginable when you were a child, so to achieve it was very exciting.

'In the modern game, young boys become affiliated to clubs at a very early age. They can be going to academies or centres of excellence at eight, nine, ten. And there are so many boys going through the system because clubs have bigger and bigger playing staffs, they seem to take on bigger youth programmes, so that a lot of young boys are either tied up with clubs or know someone at school or in the family who is at a club. By the time they get into the first team, at eighteen or nineteen, they can have been at the club for ten years. That was never the case when I was a boy. I think a lot of the mystique has gone as a result of that. Perhaps people think of football as another job, and I think that's a pity. It is a great privilege to be a professional footballer, and it's very sad that players don't live up to those expectations and those standards.'

Spoken some years before the high-profile Bowyer and Woodgate affair and others that have sullied the game's good name, Reynolds' words have a tinge of prophecy to them. But, as much as anything, they're a simple recognition of changed times and changed values. Back in the 1940s, in the aftermath of war, to be able to hold any occupation was a privilege, and codes of discipline among young men who had just come out of war work were inevitably far stricter. Equally, even the big stars of the day did not have to contend with the media intrusion that comes with today's territory, when football has migrated from back page to front. Ron and the vast majority of his playing colleagues certainly knew how to enjoy themselves, but they also had a sufficient grasp of their position as role models, and enough understanding of the sanctions that could be meted out to them should they transgress, to stick pretty much to the straight and narrow.

At this distance, and with the 1940s and 1950s dissolving into myth and legend, rose-tinted anecdotes that conceal more than they reveal, it's difficult to pronounce definitively if it was a more honest era, whether human nature was less corruptible or if the world went on much as it does now, just not in the glare of the media headlights, illuminating the murderous juggernaut hurtling towards its victims. Was Reynolds a product of the age or was he a particularly upright exception? It doesn't matter. The fact is that family and friends recall a man of outstanding integrity and honesty. In the final analysis, that's what counts. David: 'He was a total stickler for what was right and what was wrong and he was on the right side of the law. He was totally above board. He'd never do anything illegally – he'd never park illegally, never go over the speed limit, he'd pay his bills on time; just a straight, law-abiding citizen, even to the extent that for the last twenty years he wouldn't vote because he didn't believe any of the parties were any good and weren't fit to be in power! Rules were tighter then as well. He was always saying to me that he wasn't allowed to bet on the fixed odds but, because he was playing football, he never put a bet on the football pools, full stop. I used to do the pools when I was a nipper but he never said what to put down and what not to put down, he stayed totally clear of it, which is interesting in the current climate!'

Gambling on football, allowed or not, was not uppermost in Ron's thoughts back in his youth, when he was working as a draughtsman and playing a little non-league local football. The local league club was Aldershot and, by virtue of its status as an army town, during wartime it was never short of footballers, many from the higher echelons of the Football League, ready, willing and able to take the field in an Aldershot shirt as a guest. This was a common practice during the war because few players remained in one place for long. Being of prime military-service age, they generally moved from one training base to another, and so couldn't be tied to any particular club.

Once the war was over Aldershot had to build its side again; no simple task for one of the country's smaller clubs, which lay just beyond London and plenty of teams, all of which might have looked more attractive to the seasoned player. But if more experienced pros turned a blind eye to the attractions of the Recreation Ground, youngsters were far more forthcoming, so the club began to scout among the many amateur teams who played on their doorstep.

Though demotion from the Football League and immense financial problems have banished the club to the margins of the English game in more recent years, Aldershot's history goes back a long way. Like much else in the town, that story is inextricably linked to the military, since as far back as 1863 there was a football club in the town for army officers. It was another sixty-four years before a club associated with town rather than tenants came into being, however. Aldershot FC was formed just a year before Ron's birth.

Under the stewardship of the one-time Irish international William McCracken, who had learned his trade at Newcastle United, Aldershot had made good progress through the war, in no small part because of the guest players they could employ. But the reality of 'normal' life was in some ways harsher. Crowds dissipated and the 25,000-capacity ground stood virtually empty for most games. As one report of the time said, 'Present gates are too small to meet the ever growing financial requirements of a League Club . . . any help given therefore by the Supporters' Club is all the more welcome; but it explains why Aldershot must meet its deficits by parting with its most promising young players.'

If selling on your best youngsters is your only means of survival, then you'd better produce some damn good players – ask Dario Gradi at Crewe if you need confirmation. Accepting the harsh financial reality of life on a shoestring budget, McCracken was always on the lookout for new players and would always take up the recommendations of locals, either in person or via scouts, and so it was with Ron. Having been tipped the wink that here was a promising young goalkeeper, McCracken was swift to land his man. No fortunes in signing-on fees were required by the youngster.

Ron signed amateur forms with the club just as the rest of the country was recovering from VE Day and preparing for VJ Day. From August 1945, Ron began to train regularly with the Shots, and clearly he made an impression in his new surroundings. On 8 December that year he was asked to turn professional and did so, though the ever-pragmatic Reynolds also retained his job at Dennis Brothers, playing football only in a part-time capacity.

For a seventeen-year-old, it was a big step up the ladder, though not as financially lucrative as might be imagined. Ron became a pro for the princely wage of £6 14s, roughly what some clubs currently pay their scholars each week in bus fare. Of course, Ron supplemented his income with his Dennis Brothers day job. These were very different footballing days. That was further reflected in the fact that when Ron broke into the Aldershot first team, he

Debby Rapson, who discovered Ron, on his signing for Aldershot

became something of a cult hero in the locality. Football was still a sufficiently exotic profession to excite the imagination of his community, as David Reynolds explains: 'He was a local boy made good, and that made him a bit of a celebrity. People still expected to leave school and then head straight for a working life in a factory or an office and that was that. I mean, they'd never had a professional footballer who had come from this area and as a result he got relatively famous locally fairly quickly, and he had a big following. A lot of people locally used to watch him play for Aldershot.'

An early cutting from Ron's scrapbook

Fortunately for Ron and his band of followers, his Aldershot debut was not on the Recreation Ground but on the south coast at Bournemouth. The new pro put on the green jersey for the first time in January 1946.

The Football League proper was still in mothballs after the war, and regional competitions were the norm at a time when rationing continued to define English life. Injury thrust Ron into the spotlight and, after a torrid ninety minutes, he must have been pretty glad that he'd just signed up for the security of a professional contract. He saw four goals flash past him in the first forty-five minutes before things improved (slightly) in the second half and Aldershot escaped with a 7–0 beating. Their opponents *did* include Matt Busby as a guest player, though.

Things, as they say, could only get better.

CHAPTER THREE

Ron dives for a ball during one of his early first-team appearances for Aldershot at the Recreation Ground

The hardest thing for any young professional to come to terms with is the wait between signing on as a pro and earning an extended run in first-team football. This is an anxious period during which even the most confident youngster must experience more than a modicum of self-doubt. Will they ever be given the opportunity, will they be up to the task if they are, and will luck favour them? Many a promising career has been crushed by nothing more complicated than the wrong bounce of the ball or a nasty injury suffered at the wrong moment. In the face of fate, mental strength and an indomitable will are prerequisites for the successful few. Ron had these attributes in abundance.

For a goalkeeper, it's a particularly nerve-racking time, because vacancies are in such short supply. While a centre-forward might become a centre-half, or a wing-half a full-back, goalkeepers get only one shot at the team. Footballing lore also has it that goalkeepers mature late and need experience to fill the position. With that in mind, the seventeen-year-old keeper can be waiting a very long time for his opportunity.

Life in the lower leagues did and still does give budding Frank Swifts or Fabien Barthezes slightly more grounds for optimism, given the smaller clubs' penchant for playing youngsters – they're much cheaper, after all. So, while Arsenal would have been more glamourous than Aldershot, Ron was really in the ideal place when he joined his first club. Opportunity was more likely to knock on the door at the Rec. than at Highbury. Ron had plenty of opportunity to impress, but it wasn't until the 1947/48 season that he began to put an indelible mark on the Aldershot side. In that year he established himself as the regular first-choice keeper and racked up a string of superb displays. These were catalogued by the local press, and the clippings meticulously pasted into scrapbooks by Ron. Maybe the scrapbooks were a hedge against the future, revealing a nagging concern that one day soon this unexpected but exciting profession might be snatched away from Ron and he might be back to the draughtsman's desk for good. Just as it is today, football was a precarious business, and the pragmatic Reynolds must surely have worried about that. More to the point, in Ron's time you had no opportunity to build up a nice retirement nest-egg over a couple of seasons.

As it turned out, though, the scrapbooks must have acted not only as a reminder of success but almost as a CV for future employers. The Aldershot cuttings were almost uniformly enthusiastic as the young man quickly set about making a name for himself between the sticks. From the outset, Ron was a central figure in newspaper match reports once he had returned to the side after the terrible injury he sustained at Torquay at the beginning of the season. By October 1947 he was a central figure for Aldershot, and in the 2–2 draw at Newport, County's forward Mogford was 'frequently foiled by the goalkeeping of Reynolds'. The next month, at Notts County, 'Reynolds dealt confidently with the shots that came his way.' He then returned triumphant to the scene of his catastrophic debut, exorcising any ghosts in a 1–1 draw at Bournemouth. Ron

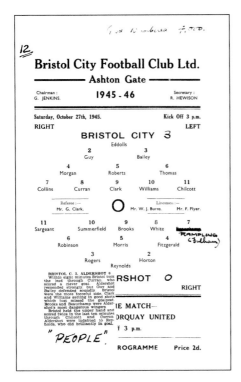

dominated the press accounts: 'Reynolds' resourceful work was a feature of the game. Twice in the second half, when McDonald and Rowell had open goals, they delayed their shots, and Reynolds rushed out to deflect the ball. It was courageous goalkeeping.'

For any youngster trying to find his feet in the league game, Aldershot was perfect. Never expected to claw their way out of the Third Division South, yet unlikely at that time to drop out of the Football League altogether, the pressure for results was far less than was the case with some of their rivals. Aldershot may have flirted with the re-election zone all season, but there was never any serious danger of the team being voted out of the Third Division South. Of course, these were the days before automatic elevation of the Conference champions (or, indeed, of the Conference itself), and non-league football was in a state of post-war disarray. This, coupled with the fact that Aldershot had themselves only recently arrived in the Football League, meant they could be fairly certain of retaining their league status, irrespective of results. With that in mind, football could be played almost for its own sake, for its own pleasures and pains. Of course, results *were* still central to the club, and ultimately to the players' chances of advancement elsewhere, but few were having sleepless nights about the outcome of a game against Swindon Town or Torquay United. If things went the wrong way, there was always next Saturday for a team which, while inconsistent, was never marooned at the foot of the table. Ron recalled, 'Aldershot was my apprenticeship, if you like, the way a carpenter or a mechanic learns his trade. Whatever job you're doing, you need to have a good understanding of the basics, and if you can learn those in a place where mistakes aren't perhaps so costly, that's ideal.'

Behind one of the division's weaker sides, Ron had plenty to keep him occupied every Saturday. And, as a young lad who'd barely ventured out of Surrey in his youth, playing for Aldershot had other compensations too, as his son David explains: 'He didn't earn a lot of money, but there was plenty of travel and a lot of experience. He went all over England, and that was just with Aldershot, because they travelled to Torquay, then they'd be up at Rotherham in the Cup, maybe even as far up country as Grimsby or Port Vale in the League. He went all over the place, so he saw a lot of the country.' Not that he and his colleagues travelled in the greatest style. Travel was usually by third-class rail – leaving players sometimes standing in crowded trains while the club directors enjoyed life in first class – or on coaches that had to traverse the country in the days before the motorway network had come into being. Occasionally, should a player be lucky enough to own a car, a bunch of his team-mates would hitch a lift.

The travelling made Christmas Day football even less palatable for the players than it might otherwise have been. Ron's first taste of festive football was up in the Midlands at Walsall, a trip that probably took four hours in each direction, in a borrowed car, because Ron couldn't afford to buy his own until he moved to Spurs several years later – a purchase he regretted, as David Reynolds recalls: 'He bought it from a vicar and it turned out to be a bum car, never worked properly. So he never trusted the clergy after that.' That nightmare trip came just five days after the season's real excitement had ended with a 2–0 defeat at Swindon in an FA Cup replay. No glamour third-round tie for the Shots, despite brilliant performances in both games from Ron. With that disappointment still fresh in the mind, what better way to spend Christmas morning than being trounced 3–0 by Walsall? 'Aldershot might have won' the match, according to the reports, but they still had to spend Christmas afternoon slogging back home to unwrap the obligatory orange in their 1940s Christmas stockings, prior to another fixture the following day.

For Ron, all of this had plenty of novelty value, of course, for in your first season in the first team everything is fresh and new, particularly when you are the player being singled out for the highest praise. At home to Reading in January he 'distinguished himself time after time', though at Loftus Road, where he had starred in a 0–0 draw, praise came laced with constructive criticism: 'In the 19-year-old Reynolds, whom Bill McCracken discovered on West Ham's doorstep, Aldershot have one of the best goalkeeping finds of the post-war years. His positional sense is good, but he needs a little more coaching in the art of handling.' That was underlined a week later in the 1–1 draw at home to Watford when, despite putting in 'stout work', it was Ron's 'only mistake that cost a goal. Stopping a free-kick from Eggleston, he dropped the ball and Thomas, quick to snap up the chance, put Watford ahead.'

For a youngster still playing part time, it was hard for Ron to put in the necessary work on his game. That said, some of his team-mates seemed to be trying to give him as much practice as they could. Opposition forwards often had licence to shoot from every angle, as in a 4–0 defeat at Exeter where 'Reynolds was much overworked. The young Aldershot goalkeeper played pluckily and well, but the odds were too great. He was beaten four times, and had not the slightest chance of preventing any of the goals.'

Despite a Football League career that was little more than six months old, Ron was starting to attract the attention of clubs far bigger than Aldershot, as they tried to fill what was becoming a problem position in the English game. Goalkeepers have always tended to have longer careers than outfielders, and so on the outbreak of war in September 1939, many of the keepers in the top flight were already into their thirties. By the time football resumed after hostilities had ended, most of them were well past their best and concluded that their footballing days were behind them. Equally, keepers who had been in their early twenties at the start of the war, the ones who were learning their trade, ready to step up into the first team in a couple of years, had found their personal development arrested by the haphazard organisation of the game through the war years. Although regional leagues were in operation, and the standard of football did remain high at times, there was certainly none of the white heat of competition that characterised peacetime league and cup games. Football was a diversion to be enjoyed rather than the matter of life and death that Bill Shankly would later espouse. Team line-ups changed constantly as guest players flitted in and out of the sides, continuity was lost and so youngsters found it hard to develop their game, often doing little more than playing in kickabouts at whichever barracks they happened to be stationed. Few had developed as they might otherwise have done, and now in their late twenties or early thirties, technical flaws that had festered uncoached and untreated for years were being shown up in the professional game. In short, while England was still living on rations, good goalkeepers were in shorter supply than almost anything else.

It was perhaps no surprise, then, that when Aldershot entertained Newport in March 1948, Burnley boss Cliff Britton was in the crowd. Britton had strong links with Aldershot, having played for them as a guest during the war. Clearly friends in the town had tipped him off about this new keeper, and he made the long trip south to see what the fuss was about. Sadly, he didn't have much time to find out, as the Reynolds injury curse struck again. Within the first half-hour Ron was stretchered off the field after he had thrown himself at the feet of Shergold, the onrushing Newport winger. The local press described it as a 'pure accident', adding that 'Reynolds was taken home by ambulance from Aldershot Hospital and subsequently went to Haslemere District Hospital for an X-ray examination. This showed his injuries are confined to bruised ribs. He was not detained in hospital and is making good progress.' Nevertheless, it was a cruel blow, and one which, temporarily at least, put a halt to Ron's hopes of improving his lot. He missed a number of matches and recaptured fitness only in time for the last couple f games of the season, by which time Britton's eye was looking elsewhere.

Perhaps reflecting on their somewhat callous treatment of Ron when he was injured at Torquay, the club this time took a more solicitous line, even keeping supporters posted on his fitness via the match programme: 'You will be glad to hear that young Reynolds' injury though serious, has turned out to be not quite so serious as first thought. X-ray has shown badly bruised ribs and back but no damage to the kidney. At the moment we are unable to say when Reynolds will be able to take his position between the sticks, but this we do say: Good luck Reynolds – thanks for all you have done for the Club during this season and for your consistent and brilliant keeping. Those of us who saw you save what looked like being a certain goal will not forget it for a long time.'

Reflecting on the 1947/48 season in the same programme, the club added, 'We started off badly with the injury to Keeper Reynolds during the first match of the season at Torquay. Once he returned to the side things brightened up and we gathered points, mainly away from home.

As if to emphasise his importance to the side, on Ron's return against Swansea at the Vetch Field, the Welsh press raved about him: 'Reynolds the Aldershot goalkeeper was undoubtedly the Man of the Match. He saved dead on shots from Powell, Dodds, Burns and McCrory, cleared repeatedly from accurate corner kicks, dived to the feet of opponents with remarkable daring, and generally covered himself with glory in a match in which the remainder of his side gave an indifferent display.'

The 1947/48 season petered out, leaving Ron to reflect on a year that had seen him prove that he was a footballer of a different class to most of those he played with and against, a goalkeeper who could play at a higher level. That Ron showed such ability beyond the norm was perhaps a greater achievement back then than it would be today. In the 1940s levels of ability were rather more even across the four divisions than they are today, when the best players are clustered not simply in the Premier League, but in the top half a dozen clubs. In these post-war years, because of the contract retention system, even if a side were to be relegated, the better players were unable simply to transfer to a new club. Even top England internationals like Tommy Lawton and Tom Finney could therefore find themselves playing for a year or two in the old Second Divison, or worse.

Playing in a lower division wasn't quite the traumatic experience it might be today, simply because all English sides played precisely the same way. Tactics never went beyond the 'WM' formation. The only change in the preceding thirty or forty years had been a subtle shift from 2–3–5 to 3–2–5, as Herbert Chapman's Arsenal in particular learned to exploit a change in the offside rule. All clubs eventually followed Chapman's lead, but none moved any further and English football stagnated tactically. At this stage, the English 'inventors of the game' were still smugly insisting that they knew all there was to know about it. Just a couple of years later that illusion was shattered in the World Cup of 1950, before being banished for ever by the visit of the Hungarians in 1953.

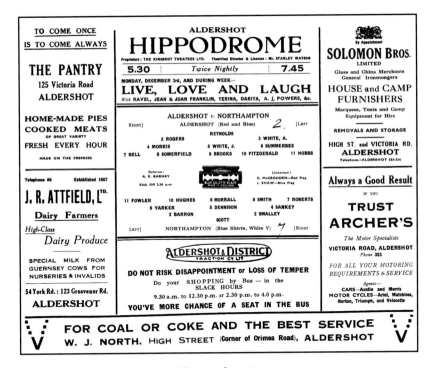

The 2-3-5 formation

However, while the difference between Aldershot and Arsenal in 1947/48 was somewhat smaller than that which currently exists between Shrewsbury and Manchester United, it was still considerable. Aldershot were a poor, struggling side even by the standards of their division, and in such circumstances, the goalkeeper has his mettle tested to the utmost. A young, inexperienced goalkeeper can expect even more of an assault. A baptism of fire it may have been, but it was a helpful one for all that. Looking back at that year, Ron delivered his summary in the margins of an early scrapbook, typically putting the team's performance before his own:'For the team this was a very poor season. Once again only just succeeded in getting away from the re-election zone. However, personally, the season has been a great success, apart from two nasty injuries, which necessitated the missing of 10 matches. I feel myself that I have at last been able to do something. I have just started to benefit from the past three seasons' experience. For this I have to thank many for their most valuable advice at all times. Total of first-team appearances to date for the past three seasons 86.'

So many first-team games at the age of twenty merely reinforced local opinion that Reynolds wasn't long for the parochial Aldershot world. But that was reckoning without the draconian restrictions of a player's contract. Ron Reynolds would be bonded to Aldershot for quite a while to come.

CHAPTER FOUR

FOOTBALL LEAGUE (SOUTH)							
	P.	W.	D.	L.	For	Ag.	Pts.
Cardiff City	11	8	0	3	47	18	16
Crystal Palace ...	11	7	2	2	27	18	16
Bristol City	13	7	1	5	29	28	15
Bristol Rovers ...	11	6	1	4	25	23	13
Bournemouth & B. ...	12	5	2	5	37	30	12
Swindon Town ...	10	5	2	3	19	16	12
ALBION	13	6	0	7	31	36	12
Aldershot	13	3	4	6	23	40	10
Exeter City	12	3	3	6	22	24	9
Torquay United ...	11	2	3	6	12	34	7
Reading	11	2	2	7	22	27	6

OFFICIAL ATTENDANCE

HOME		AWAY	
Cardiff ...	9,294	Cardiff ...	22,000
Total to date		Total to date	

A typical League position for Aldershot

We live in altered footballing times; so altered that you wonder if most members of the football establishment have traded Delia Smith's cookbooks for the more exotic recipes of Timothy Leary. When an eighteen-year-old like Jermaine Jenas can move up to the Premiership for £5 million after fewer than fifty First Division appearances – having spent most of his short life in the football academy system, and with an agent already by his side – it's small wonder that these youngsters view the game as a career choice, just as they might view merchant banking, DJing or graphic design. When money moves in, poetry moves out and the loss of football's innocence has come at a price; too great a price for the traditionalists among us.

In the days of Ron Reynolds' youth, few thought of football as a career; a job, yes, a privileged job even, but never a career. It was simply something that, if you had the talent, you could do for ten years, hopefully amassing enough cash to open a sports shop, or set yourself up as a pub landlord once the boots were finally hung up.

For all that Ron loved the game, he never believed it would be the central focus of his life, as he once explained: 'Young players now, if they've got a bit of ability, even not much ability, they get swallowed up by football clubs when they're just children. And if they carry on impressing coaches and so on, then they're well looked after, they go into these academies or whatever they want to call them, and it's like a prodigy going into a university years ahead of their time to study physics or mathematics. It's a hothouse and, of course, some of these young boys fall by the wayside. But football seems to be the focus of everything to them and I think they lose sight of the fact that it's a game, and they lose the enjoyment of it. And that's a shame, especially if they join a big club very early. That carries a lot of responsibility even for the young boys and I think that they're always aware that money plays a very big part in everything they do; that a lot of money rests on what they do in the future.

'I never had that when I was coming into the game. I carried on learning a trade outside football because that was what you did then. Even if you succeeded as a player, you always thought you'd have to go back to a proper job when you were in your thirties, so you got a trade. Playing football and getting paid a few pounds for it was a bonus, it really was, and so there was a lot less thinking about: If I move here, then in two years I can move there and I'll make that amount of money and get into that division.

'Really, I think that for most of the players − and I except the great players, people like Greaves or Bobby Charlton, Edwards or Finney, people who had such great ability that they were always going to be at the top − but most of us were happy to be playing the game and to see where it took us. It was something of an adventure really. Even playing league football we got to see places we wouldn't have otherwise, and I suppose that meant we were happy to see things take their course. Perhaps we were less personally ambitious than players are today, but that was no bad thing.

'That's why I probably stayed at Aldershot longer than I needed to when I was starting out in the game, because I enjoyed it, and because I was training as a draughtsman. Later, of course, it was because Aldershot wouldn't let me go!'

Perhaps that measured assessment was the result of time dulling the edge of ambition, or perhaps it was simply that Ron came into football at a time when your lot was set out for you. As a youth, at least, he found it easier to accept, rather than challenge, the status quo. That was one characteristic that would disappear completely within a few short years, though.

An early Aldershot line-up

As it was, barely into his twenties, Ron was enjoying making a name for himself. But, Ron being Ron, and Ron being the fearless keeper that he was, it wasn't all plain sailing. With Aldershot desperate to improve on the season that had seen them finish nineteenth of twenty-two, and only a single point ahead of the three beneath them – Bristol Rovers, Norwich City and Brighton and Hove Albion – a good start was essential. Instead, the 1948/49 season began with a mixed afternoon.

Aldershot opened with a 1–1 draw at home to Leyton Orient, not earth shattering, but solid. For Ron, however, it was another season opener ruined by injury caused by a run-in with an opposing forward on the bone-hard August ground: 'Reynolds had to receive attention after a collision with McGeachy, and played with a bandage over his right eye for the rest of the game. He threw clear, then fell on his back ten yards from the goal . . . [He] had a stitch inserted over his right eye after the game.' Business as usual.

A mere flesh wound wasn't going to stop Ron in his tracks, and within three weeks he was saving a first-minute Exeter penalty in a 'resourceful display' that still couldn't prevent the Shots dropping more home points in a 1–2 defeat. But if Ron was starting to feel that the season was going rapidly downhill, a 0–4 win at Brighton looked to have turned the tide, leaving him to enjoy 'the quietest afternoon he has ever experienced at the coast resort'. Luck was also on Aldershot's side a few days later when they beat Southend 1–0 at home, even though 'Southend staged a storming finish and Reynolds saved a point in the last ten minutes.' However, the day was best remembered for the presence of some pre-match entertainment, proving that the mascot isn't merely a modern-day scourge but one that spans the decades, as the press reported: 'Before the game Pop Littlewood, 82, oldest and one of the keenest supporters, introduced the Club's original mascot to the crowd. This midget footballer in the Aldershot colours was making his first public appearance for some years and may have helped [Aldershot captain] Sheppard to win the toss.'

Just as ancient a phenomenon is the depressed fan, demanding to learn why it is that his team is so dismal. After Ron had been one of the few to enhance his reputation in a 2–0 defeat at Northampton Town, Major E. Bough was forced to write a letter of complaint to the local press: 'Today I feel I must ask the directors a question: What's wrong with our team? There is definitely something wrong. There can only be one of three things: management, training, or esprit de corps. Get these three things straightened out and you get a team. As I see it, the boys have got it there, but don't, for some reason, give it. Why? I have told you, now you tell me! Is the management carried out in the right manner? Does the team train for their arduous work? If so, how, when and where and what? Is the spirit there that carries a team to victory?'

In other words, sack the manager. *Plus ça change . . .*

Similarly consistent was Ron, back from his injury and playing a Canute-like role in goal, though a bit more successfully than the tidally obsessed king managed. In October, though Aldershot slipped to a 2–0 defeat at Reading, the home side's tally 'might well have reached double figures judging by the number of scoring chances the Reading forwards had . . . Reynolds, in brilliant form in Aldershot's goal, stole the limelight. Shots rained in on him from an inspired attack, and he undoubtedly saved his side from a heavier defeat. Brilliant as was his work, Reynolds should have been beaten more than twice by the Reading forwards.'

Understandably, playing at the lowest level of the senior game, Ron often found himself confronted by forwards who weren't of the highest calibre, but that was not always the case. The maximum wage might have been a scandal insofar as it artificially depressed the amount of money players could earn, but it did mean that the weekly pay packets at Tottenham and Torquay were broadly similar. So, for example, it didn't raise too many eyebrows to see Tommy Lawton, one of the greatest English centre-forwards, toiling away in the lower divisions with Notts County towards the end of his career. Inevitably, County were regarded as something of a goal machine when Aldershot visited Meadow Lane in October 1948.

According to Ron, 'Football has lost something with players moving about so much. Supporters can't have the same relationship with the players if they're here today, gone tomorrow. You can't have heroes in that way. You had people like Jimmy Dickinson who was at Portsmouth for many years, Billy Wright at Wolves, Ray Barlow at West Brom, and, OK, they were successful clubs. But you had it lower down the league too, and every club had its stalwarts whom they could depend on. That's going out of the game and I think that breaks a link between players and supporters.'

Like most sides of the time, County put the emphasis on attack, and even though they ultimately finished in mid-table in the Third Division South, people were flocking to see them. It reached a point when County were struggling to pack in the legions of supporters. They were finally required to issue this heartfelt plea in their match-day programme: 'We repeat our previous request to ALL SUP-PORTERS. Please pack together as closely as possible. We require your utmost co-operation in this matter, for without it we cannot possibly accommodate the numbers who wish to see our matches. We are submitting plans for the immediate rebuilding of our Spion Kop, and subject to the same being approved we shall commence work almost immediately. Please do not read this notice and then ignore it. Keep the corners clear, pack as closely as possible and obey the instructions of any police officer in uniform immediately.'

It looks laughable now, but the 'sardines policy' that existed then, and persisted for a further forty years, was putting us on the inevitable road to the disasters at Bolton, Ibrox and Hillsborough, as football clubs looked for every way to squeeze an extra few pennies out of every game, and never mind the consequences.

On the field the Lawton menace was enough to see County through to a 2–0 win, but, again, it was Ron who caught the eye of the press, who paid tribute to his 'gallant work in the second half, when Lawton & Co. were all out for goals . . . Reynolds dealt effectively with all manner of shots and earned the applause of the large crowd, one of his saves from Lawton bearing the stamp of first-class goalkeeping . . . the brilliance of Reynolds not only upset the Notts County scoring machine but also inspired his colleagues to fight back.' Just not quite hard enough.

Ron was still earning the princely sum of £6 a week for his work with the Shots; 'earning' was still the key word, since the team was as riddled with defensive holes as it had been in the previous season. Time and again Ron won the plaudits from the press, despite being in a losing team and forced to pick the ball out of the net with grim regularity. Scouts continued to take an interest in his progress, with representatives from Everton and Aston Villa in the crowd when Aldershot went down 1–2 at home to Swansea. The game nevertheless moved one reporter to write, 'Reynolds could easily be an international in the making.'

The big boys still bided their time, though, and Ron continued to learn his trade at Aldershot, which at least gave him an early opportunity to play in the FA Cup that season. Fortune favoured him this time around as the club visited Portman Road to take on a vastly superior Ipswich side. Having dominated for much of the game, Ipswich enjoyed a 1–0 lead early in the second half, though that could have been more after a rare Reynolds clanger. Blinded by the sunlight, he dropped a shot that was scrambled off the line by a colleague. On the hour mark and with Aldershot on the way out, 'waves of fog swept up from the river, and in five minutes converted the bright sunshine into a black-out'. In these pre-floodlight days the game could not continue and was abandoned. Aldershot returned to Suffolk the next week and thumped the home side 0–3. Man of the match? Ron Reynolds.

'A superb exhibition of goalkeeping by Reynolds was the outstanding feature of this Cup tie replay in which Aldershot registered a three-goal win entirely against the run of the game. It's little wonder that several First Division clubs are watching Reynolds. Week after week it's his daring and brilliant positioning that features in Aldershot's game, and this Cup tie should be clearly labelled Reynolds' game.

'During long periods, Reynolds was in action incessantly. He saved from all Ipswich forwards in turn and his finest effort was to turn away a penalty kick at a time when neither side had scored and a goal for Ipswich might have made all the difference to the subsequent course of the game.

'Ipswich did not reach last week's form, but it was undoubtedly Reynolds who won the game for Aldershot. But fortune smiles on those who help themselves, and, apart from anyone else, Ron Reynolds gave us our money's worth by his grand exhibition of goalkeeping.

'Manager Bill McCracken thinks he has the best young goalkeeper in the country in Reynolds. And Ipswich supporters who saw their own team beaten 3–0 in the FA Cup will probably agree. Reynolds was brilliant.'

There was little doubt that Ron was the coming man in the Third Division South, perhaps the biggest talent on show at the time, and there was no disguising the way in which he was coveted by clubs with plenty more to offer than Aldershot ever could, in honours if

Another penalty to deal with

not finance. Yet the move away from the Recreation Ground was still elusive, due to an odd cocktail of Aldershot's intransigence and Ron's own lack of ambition, at least insofar as football was concerned.

As the footballing bush telegraph began to hum with stories of Ron's qualities, the local press began to put out stories designed to dampen the interest of the big boys. It was suggested that Ron would never dream of leaving the comfort of the Recreation Ground because he had his mind fixed on other things, as one newspaper suggested in its New Year's Day look ahead to 1949:

'After a close study I find there are few really outstanding defenders [in the Third Division]. Among goalkeepers Aldershot have probably one of the youngest and best in Reynolds, but he may never get to the top for the reason he has decided to make football secondary to his business career.'

Prefiguring tabloid practices that would become sadly commonplace thirty years later, this report was a masterpiece of disinformation, taking a germ of truth and manipulating it to a point where it was barely recognisable. Certainly Ron had never ruled out further progress in the game: 'My attitude was that I wanted to continue studying for my profession, but that that didn't mean I had to stay in Aldershot. Had I been offered a transfer to some club such as Watford or Swindon or Reading, clubs not much bigger than ours and with no better prospects, then I don't think it would have been worth my while and I would have continued at Aldershot. But when they were talking about the likes of Everton, or, later on, Arsenal, then I don't think anybody would refuse that. So it would be true to say that I wasn't actively seeking a move, I didn't do that until later, but had a good transfer come about, my other career wouldn't have prevented me moving.'

It was inevitable that Aldershot would want to keep Ron, especially as they had lost Alf Rowland, their excellent centre-half, at the tail end of 1948, when he had finally taken the opportunity to move on.

When the Shots crashed out of the FA Cup, losing 3–1 to Gateshead of the Third Division North, things came close to crisis point at the Hampshire club, with the supporters in what passed for open revolt in those days.

'Complaints against a few spectators who shout words of abuse of a most discouraging nature to the Aldershot players were mentioned by Mr A. V. Barraclough, Chairman of Aldershot FC, when addressing the crowd over the loudspeaker system before Saturday's match against Watford.

'He appealed to those concerned to refrain from this objectionable practice and said that several players had approached him and he was convinced that these comments made in a loud voice, had disheartened them very much. Mr Barraclough added a reminder that the Football Association take a serious view of such incidents.

'Referring to Rowland's transfer, he said his co-directors had parted with their popular centre-half only after giving full consideration to his request, and to his interests and ambitions. He believed that every supporter would share wholeheartedly their opinion that

Rowland had fully deserved this recognition and promotion.'

Rowland's transfer, along with the fickle nature of the crowd, certainly began to sow seeds in Ron's mind. There's no question that in the latter stages of the 1948/49 season Ron began to consider the possibility of asking to leave seriously for the first time, so that he may further his footballing career. He had married in July 1947 and, having enlisted the help of his family to persuade his wife to stay at home rather than go out to work, it was clearly his responsibility to ensure that a decent wage was coming into the house. But he was too busy to do anything about a move immediately. Somebody had to keep Aldershot in the Football League.

That had been something that had worried fans of Brighton the previous season. However, despite finishing bottom of the Third Division South, they were re-elected to league membership and were making the most of it with a sustained promotion bid. Then, as now, glory hunters didn't limit themselves to following Manchester United, and people were hopping on the Brighton bandwagon in force, according to the Aldershot press. '"Success brings the crowd" is a football truism. Brighton's success this season has added quite 7,000 to last season's normal attendances, and they will bring more than 500 supporters to Aldershot, the Supporters' Club having chartered a special train. So keen were they to see last Saturday's game at Swansea that the Supporters' Club asked British Railways whether they could buy a train for the day and charge their own fares. The answer was no, but 50 supporters travelled at the ordinary return fare of 46 shillings. Another party chartered an aeroplane.'

Their trek to Aldershot was less taxing, and less pleasing, as they were held to a 1–1 draw, thanks to a penalty save from Ron. The spot-kick had been awarded in controversial circumstances: 'Aldershot fans howled when Referee R. Tarratt (Horsham) awarded a last-minute penalty to Brighton. One sporting hoodlum went further. "I was struck on my way to the dressing room," complained Mr Tarratt.' And that was in the 'good old days'.

The outburst came after Aldershot had been treated to some

Opposite page *Ron keeps Millwall at bay, January and December 1949 (Empics)*

great sportsmanship just days earlier by Millwall fans (clearly this period belonged in some parallel universe). Ron was again star of the show in a 1–1 draw in which he 'dealt with all sorts of shots, high shots, low shots that sent the ball skidding at great pace on the muddy surface from which the ball had to be caught in one out-stretched hand. All were stopped after the manner of a master. In spasmodic raids Reynolds in the Aldershot goal was seldom called upon, but when he was he showed marked confidence and wonder-ful agility in getting to the ball.' In the aftermath, a number of Millwall fans wrote to the Shots to say they'd put on the best display they'd seen all season, with one correspondent from Stratford employing the language of Shakespeare to eulogise, 'Your team gained a point that was thoroughly deserved and I shall not com-plain if the Lions drop points at home to visitors regularly, providing we receive the same entertainment as supplied by your team on Saturday. Good Luck, Aldershot, your lowly position is false.'

Reporting these letters in the press, the local reporter added the barbed comment that 'These spontaneous tributes may provide a clue to the reason for Aldershot's more convincing displays in away games than on the Recreation Ground, where more encourage-ment and less criticism from the spectators might prove helpful.'

Gradually, Aldershot made their future safe, despite collecting two points fewer than in 1948/49. They avoided bottom place in the table thanks to the incompetence of Crystal Palace, who ended six points adrift (and that was well before Trevor Francis ever got hold of them). For all that, Aldershot was simply a club marking time, scratching out a living in the lower reaches of the Third Division South with no clear plan, nor even any ambition, of scaling the table.

With praise coming out of his ears, it was no wonder that Ron began to feel his time in Hampshire was up, especially when he read comments attributed to manager Bill McCracken that said he was 'convinced Reynolds is booked for England honours'. Ron's was the name that dominated in the team's press. In February it was sug-gested that 'By the trend of things, Aldershot will soon have nearly as many scouts as spectators at their matches. Ron Reynolds, the young goalkeeper whose safe hands and amazing judgement have rocketed him into the five-figure class, is the main target.'

The crux of the matter was that football was evolving quickly. In the past, talented youngsters had been able to ply their trade in the basement divisions and yet still gain international recognition of one sort or another. But after the war, the bigger clubs in the land began to flex their muscles, and the selection committee that presented England boss Walter Winterbottom with the fait accompli of the national team had started to concentrate its attentions on a handful of clubs who were challenging for the League Championship and FA Cup on a regular basis. As one contemporary report put it, 'The club that lands Reynolds will have a potential international. Quick as a cat, he takes excellent position, and his handling of the ball puts him in the Frank Swift class. But here comes the rub, and the most important factor, possibly, in the slower development of young players to-day: to progress a lad must get to one of the clubs in the higher divisions. If he stays with a Third Division club, he usually stands still or goes back.'

Blackpool appeared the club most likely to win Ron's signature, which would have put him in a team that fielded the likes of Matthews and Mortensen and might have seen him on his way to a part in the immortal Matthews Cup Final of 1953.

The only problem was Aldershot weren't selling.

TOTTENHAM HOTSPUR

CHAPTER FIVE

Growth is the essential element of life – if you're not growing, you're decaying. For the most part, growth is admired, welcomed even. Except when you're outgrowing your immediate surroundings, and then it often becomes a source of real resentment. Nowhere is that truer than in professional football, where growth can upset the delicate balance, particularly in a team that is looking to move forward and improve its lot.

Any football team starting from a low base needs a focal player or two around which to build; players clearly more talented than the majority of their colleagues. By virtue of their skill, they can drag the club up to a higher level, on to a new plane, as Paul Merson has done recently at both Middlesbrough and Portsmouth. Unfortunately, the very fact that they are more talented than their colleagues brings a raft of difficulties. Struggling teams will, in general, build on a youth policy, so the next generation of players has the responsibility of propelling the side forward. Obviously, these youngsters have greater personal ambition than those in their late twenties or early thirties, who have generally found their level by that stage of their careers. Those in their teens or early twenties are far more likely to be looking to play at a higher level. If their less gifted team-mates can't help them achieve that, then, in general, they'll be looking for a new club that can. And if they leave, so do the club's hopes of moving on to the next level. Just imagine where Crewe could be now had they managed to retain all the gems that Dario Gradi has uncovered there over the years. But, because individual ambition and the club's finances have made progress impossible, Crewe's horizons extend little further than a place in the lower reaches of the First Division.

In the summer of 1949 Ron Reynolds had clearly outgrown his team-mates and his club and was in danger of stagnating if he stayed at Aldershot. But, for the club, already under fire from disgruntled fans, the sale of Reynolds would be just another indicator that the board had concluded that Aldershot had gone as far as they were going to go. So the club simply declared that they were retaining Ron's registration for the 1949/50 season, and that was an end to the matter.

Aldershot did have one advantage over their present-day counterparts. While money may have been tight, there were few of the strains on cash flow that exist today. Players' wages were pegged tightly – Ron's salary for 1949/50 touched the giddy heights of £7 10s per week – and crowds continued to be much larger than at the bulk of Third Division games today, with Aldershot averaging a gate of around seven thousand in the five months to Christmas 1949. Having also sold Rowland the year before, Aldershot's board had no financial need to offload any other player and every political reason to keep hold of their prime asset.

This was fine for the club, but Ron was growing increasingly impatient with the team's failings. He was also increasingly confident in his own talent, reminded of it as he was on a weekly basis by the gentlemen of the press, and certainly ready to test himself against better opposition. He felt he had finished his apprenticeship and now was the time for him to put his ability to the test.

In almost every game he played, wherever he went, he found himself the focus of attention. And he didn't disappoint, putting in a string of great performances that caught the eye of football fans throughout the south in particular. He was even mentioned in the letters pages of one national newspaper when the Footballer of the Year awards were announced. Mr A.J. Carter of Herne Bay thought that the elevation of Manchester United's captain, Johnny Carey, was evidence of an unhealthy concentration upon the upper reaches of English football, while the lower leagues were left to atrophy, starved of the oxygen of publicity. Does that sound familiar? Mr Carter wrote, 'I would like other readers' views on the choosing of Footballer of the Year. I have often wondered how he is chosen. I see that it was Carey this year, and while admitting that he is undoubtedly a great player, is it always necessary for a First Division player to hold the title?

'I am a supporter of a Third Division club, and it does seem to me that a player who is consistently brilliant is justly entitled to be called the Footballer of the Year. One player who has greatly impressed me this season is Reynolds, the Aldershot goalkeeper. Against my team he gave one of the finest displays of intelligent goalkeeping that I have seen in over 35 years' experience.

'Every week when reading a report of Aldershot's matches it would seem to be the same. Always a brilliant performance by Reynolds. Considering that Aldershot as a team have such a poor playing record, he must indeed be a very fine player. I am quoting this man as an example of what I mean. There must be some Third Division players just as entitled to the honour as the usual chosen few.'

Ron's profile was being boosted regularly by mentions such as this and, aware that he was coveted by other clubs, during the 1949 summer, he made his first tentative enquiry about the possibility of leaving Aldershot. He was told by the club that had lauded Rowland's ambition that he was going nowhere and the matter was not up for discussion.

As Oscar Wilde said, 'I can resist everything except temptation', and, for Ron, knowing that the big-name clubs were sniffing around must have made it even harder to bear when Aldershot turned down his transfer request. It was common knowledge that Arsenal were especially keen on him, though one of their representatives was heard to ask, 'Isn't he a little daring?' Whether that was a reference to his penchant for picking up injuries in brave, if sometimes foolhardy, challenges isn't clear, but even if Arsenal were hesitating, there were at least two other suitors: the aforementioned Blackpool, said to be ready with a big offer, and Manchester City, who saw Ron as a possible successor to the great Frank Swift – high praise indeed. Aldershot couldn't escape the interest in Reynolds, even at a Football League meeting, when manager Bill McCracken was tapped up by a number of managers who made enquiries about Ron's availability. If there were any hope of horse-trading re-election votes in exchange for Ron's signature, McCracken put a stop to it. Ron was going nowhere.

Given such intransigence on the part of the club, Ron's bizarre start to the season might have been put down to petulance. In many other players it would have been. For Ron, however, it was a thoroughly embarrassing accident. Missing his train to head up to Fellows Park for the season's opener at Walsall, Ron had to jump into a borrowed car and make the 150-mile drive from Haslemere to the Midlands, constantly battling against time. In those blissful pre-mobile-phone days it was hard to keep tabs on Ron's progress on his pilgrimage north. McCracken was therefore left with a hard decision to make, especially as substitutues were still well in the future. Unbelievably, McCracken gambled on Ron arriving in time and handed in a team sheet with his name on it. Kick-off time arrived but Ron hadn't. Putting left-back Dick Jales in goal, Aldershot took to the field with just ten men, and managed to keep Walsall out for the first fifteen minutes until Ron arrived, got changed and ran on to the pitch to ironic applause. Typically, he then went on to underline the wisdom of McCracken's decision, seeing Aldershot through to a 0–0 draw with 'a succession of masterly saves [that] more than anything else earned Aldershot a point'.

McCracken's faith emphasised the great understanding he had with Reynolds, and vice versa. McCracken clearly viewed Ron as a prodigy and protégé, while Ron was only too keen to learn from a man who had been in the game all his life and possessed a sharp, original brain. McCracken was always willing to try the unusual in an effort to get his messages across. In the case of Ron, he leaned heavily on the fact that Ron had a career outside football, and, better yet, one that could be actively applied to his on-field education. Knowing that Ron was a draughtsman, that he had an excellent grasp of mathematics and a bright, enquiring mind, McCracken saw an invaluable opportunity to teach positional sense, as the manager explained to the journalist James Connolly: 'He grasped the importance of angles immediately. Then we went to work not on the field, but in the office on pieces of paper. I showed him the angles at which a goalkeeper was vulnerable as he advanced from goal, and how to narrow them down. Afterwards we went on the field and practised. The secret of Reynolds' remarkable keeping is simply that before he advances to intercept an opposing player, he quickly assesses the safe angle of interception with the skilled eye of a mathematician.' That work was to prove invaluable and was a skill that was passed down the family later, as Ron's son David remembers:

'Dad was always talking about making sure you knew your angles, knew where your goal was. He was very meticulous in marking out his area, which has been outlawed recently. He'd mark a line from the goalposts out to the six-yard line, and then a line back from the penalty spot to the goal as well, so that he could see exactly where he was in relation to the net behind him. He always stressed how important that was because it was a big part of his game. It enabled him to be very quick off his line, something that he always made a big point about in coaching, and something in which he was really ahead of his time. In his day, most goalkeepers would stay at home on the line. His training as a draughtsman taught him to think in three dimensions and he brought that back to his game.'

While McCracken enjoyed Ron's full confidence, the home crowd was less sanguine, giving a vote of apathy to the players and their admittedly lukewarm performances. Was it the job of the crowd to back the team, or the job of the team to excite the paying public? One correspondent to the local press, D. W. Fluck, was in no doubt: 'No team can win every match, and anyone can support a winning team, but I would suggest that each member of the public who attends the next home game decides to give 100 per cent. Vocal SUPPORT to the boys all the time, and then continue to do the same each and every game afterwards. Then, and only then, will we see a successful team, for at the moment the local crowd does not deserve the success it asks for!'

Blaming the crowd wasn't really an option for the board and management at Aldershot. Instead, they fell back on the old chestnut of pleading poverty: complaining that the financial position of the club was such that they could not hope to compete in the transfer market, arguing that with gates falling, special measures were necessary. Just a few years after the country had been asked to do its bit for the war effort, the Aldershot board declared that the club's future was in the hands of the supporters. The Aldershot Football Club Development Fund was therefore launched after lengthy talks with the general committee of the Supporters' Club. A statement declared that: 'In view of the fact that the Football Club's problems are mainly of a financial nature it was the considered opinion that a partial solution might be found by: (1) Further and spontaneous financial assistance by the Supporters' Club on the clear understanding that this would be a help, but would not necessarily solve all the problems. (2) A united effort to raise a substantial sum as a gift to Aldershot Football Club, so that the directors can be more progressive in their efforts to provide attractive football and contribute to the amenities on behalf of the town and surrounding districts.'

With the need for cash so apparent, Ron took this as a signal that Aldershot might be ready to part with him, and responded with a series of superb performances. Manchester City's scouts were again scurrying south to take a look at the Swift potential of the young man.

Ron's ability was being discussed by several influential commentators, notably Charles Buchan, former England and Arsenal leader, and one of the most important writers about the game in the country. His opinion mattered, and his opinion was that 'Ron Reynolds is now in the Frank Swift class.'

Once again, Reading suffered at Ron's hands as Aldershot raced to a 1–3 win at Elm Park. When saving an early penalty, Ron leaped 'like a panther to the right, flung out his arm and punched the ball

In action at Selhurst Park, October 1949

out for a corner. It was a magnificent save, and Reynolds deserved the ovation from the crowd. For the rest of the game this young goalkeeper twisted, turned and caught the ball cleanly in the air.'

The pace off the field quickened now, as, once again denied a transfer, Ron took matters into his own hands, as David Reynolds recalls: 'He knew he was doing well and he knew he was being watched, getting noticed. So he realised that he needed to get to a bigger club. Aldershot wouldn't give him a transfer so he wrote to about half a dozen big clubs: Tottenham, Arsenal, West Brom, Birmingham, Villa, Southampton.' There were also letters to Manchester City. This was a highly unorthodox move on Ron's part, and, some might say, of dubious morality, given the times. But then it was hardly any more dubious than the practice of retaining a player's contract even if he wanted to move on to progress.

If Ron were disenchanted with his lot, that was nothing when compared with the Aldershot supporters, who continued either to voice their displeasure or vote with their feet. As ever, two distinct factions sprung up: those who felt that once they'd paid their money they could do as they liked; and those who characterised themselves as loyal supporters. The latter group rallied around in the pages of the local press. One such was H.G. Stone: 'If transfer fees were possible for club supporters, those of Aldershot would not command a very high figure. There is a small loyal core but too much of the "If they don't win, I shan't go" spirit. Lots more enthusiasm and more vocal encouragement would, I am sure, produce the same football the boys play away.' C. Ireson of Farnham attacked the boo-boys even more harshly yet, writing: 'A more ungenerous crowd of supporters I have yet to meet.'

Around the turn of the year, a crisis point was reached, and after twelve and a half years Bill McCracken handed in his notice and left the club. Ron's determination to leave the Recreation Ground clearly intensified on hearing the news. As soon as McCracken was out of the door, another transfer request made its way to the board. Finally giving in to the inevitable, this time the board said yes. The new manager, Gordon Clark, had not even been appointed.

Given Ron's door-to-door selling of himself, and the obvious interest that there had been in him earlier in the season, he must have assumed that a move was a matter of days or at worst weeks away, but he was to endure a frustrating hiatus that would see him have to wait out the rest of the season. Looking back, Ron believed that, 'Although they granted the transfer, I don't think they ever had any intention of selling me before the end of the season. In those days, a club didn't have to tell you if there'd been any interest in you or not. It was entirely up to them, which was crazy. It was your career, but they didn't have to tell you anything, you were completely bound to the club.'

Aldershot's flirtation with the bottom spot in the division went on to the last day of the season. They were saved by a run-in of three wins and a draw in the last four games of the season, with just one goal conceded, and finished two points clear of Millwall. The final game was a thumping 5–0 win over Ipswich. It was fitting that Ron kept a clean sheet in that match at the Recreation Ground. It was his 167th first-team appearance for the Shots. It was also his last.

CHAPTER SIX

Ron had more than proved that he was a young man of considerable patience. He'd remained at Aldershot for a season or more than his rapid development as a player had warranted, and then sat through those last, difficult months of the 1949/50 season once his transfer had been granted. Understandably, he went into the summer of 1950 in fairly low spirits, and admitted that he had begun to question whether the move he wanted would ever materialise. Perhaps all the rumours of top-flight scouts following his progress had been nothing more than talk. Perhaps they'd simply been keeping tabs on him as a matter of course, of routine, rather than with any great intent.

In spite of the letters Ron had sent to clubs up north, Haslemere remained his home. Son David had been born in March 1950, so, in hindsight, the fact that no transfer came to pass during that period was probably a blessing, preventing upheaval at an already fraught time. Away from home, Ron remained a leading light in the local community, opening the batting and keeping wicket for the Shottermill Cricket Club. Clearly, despite the wandering nature of some of his ancestors, Ron had set down real roots. Which was just as well, because when he reported back for pre-season training at the Recreation Ground, it looked very much like he might be at Aldershot for the duration of another relegation-haunted term. He was, however, phlegmatic about that possibility: 'If you're a professional, in whatever walk of life it is, then you should do your job to the very best of your ability all the time. You're being paid to do that, so you should give value for that money, or you shouldn't take it.'

But preparation for the new season had barely got under way when, according to David Reynolds, his dad's life was changed for ever: 'One day in July that year, the chairman of Aldershot approached him and just said to him, "There's a London club been after you, they want to talk to you, I've told them that you're going to go up and visit them, you're going to be at Waterloo Station at such and such a time." So, even then, although he wanted to leave Aldershot to better himself, he really had no say in it. They were told where to go, when to go, what to do, and I know he wasn't happy about that side of things, the way players were treated by clubs.'

Worse yet, the Aldershot chairman barely gave Ron any of the facts surrounding the deal he had already cooked up for his transfer. When he set off for Waterloo Station, all Ron knew was that he was heading for talks with a London club: it might have been Chelsea, it might have been Orient, for all he knew. By a process of elimination, working back through the clubs he knew had been following his progress in the previous season, Ron finally concluded that he was off for talks with Arsenal. So it came as something of a surprise when he found himself discussing a possible transfer with Jimmy Anderson, the assistant manager at Tottenham Hotspur.

This shows how far footballers have come in fifty years. When fans complain that players have too much power, too much money, too much everything, those that were the victims of such blatant exploitation probably exclaim, 'About time too!' Never mind footballers, can anyone imagine going to a job interview without knowing which company it is, yet knowing that all the contractual details have been resolved well in advance without your participation? Suddenly the footballer's agent doesn't seem quite the ogre, does he?

When Ron headed for Waterloo, it was to a virtual fait accompli. Ultimately, he could turn down the move and stay with Aldershot. But if he took that course who knew what the Shots' reaction would be? They might hold on to his registration in future years and deny him a move, or even match action. Similarly, there was no going to the meeting with an open mind, hearing what his suitor had to say and then waiting for an auction to begin. It wasn't up to the player to decide where he went: the club told him where he was going. Once Tottenham had come up with a deal acceptable to Aldershot – the details of which remained shrouded in secrecy – the Third Division club had no need to look elsewhere, or to wait on other bids. All they were interested in was getting the cash into the coffers. As it turned out, the fee itself was fairly small, a mere £3,000. But Aldershot received Spurs' outside-left Ken Flint as part of the deal. It was ultimately a successful swap for him given that he racked up 70 goals in more than 300 appearances for the Shots.

The crux of the matter, however, was Ron's choice. Getting over his initial surprise at meeting Jimmy Anderson rather than a representative dispatched from the marble halls of Highbury, Ron quickly got down to business, 'over a currant bun and a cup of tea in the old cafeteria at Waterloo! I was taken aback by Tottenham's interest in me, because I hadn't had any real indication that they were one of the teams watching me closely. And so far as Spurs went, they weren't as attractive an option as Arsenal at that time, because they'd only just got promotion from the Second Division that season, where Arsenal had finished only four points from the top of the First Division.' In spite of that, or perhaps because of it, Ron quickly warmed to the idea of a switch to White Hart Lane, particularly once the club made it clear that they had no objection to him continuing to live in Haslemere and travelling up to training by car. The very fact that Tottenham had come from Division Two suggested that Ron might have more opportunities to play first-team football, even though Spurs had Ted Ditchburn as their international-class promotion-winning keeper. Ron certainly didn't underestimate Ditchburn's qualities as a goalkeeper, but with him nudging thirty, there was the likelihood that he might begin to pick up more injuries. Certainly that was the view within the corridors of power at Spurs, with manager Arthur Rowe desperately keen to find a capable deputy for their return to the top flight.

Rowe was the key man in Ron's move to Spurs, even though he wasn't present that day at Waterloo. As something of a footballing purist, Reynolds was far more taken with the style of play on offer under Rowe than that played by Arsenal. Having seen the Gunners play at Fratton Park the previous season, Ron was thoroughly unimpressed, writing in his diary, 'Very poor game!' The more functional, robust Arsenal style, while undeniably effective, didn't strike a chord with young Ron, while Spurs' outlook, based on quick interpassing and fluent attacking moves from back to front vividly caught his imagination.

The 'push-and-run' style that Rowe was busily implementing was based in part on the continental model that would sweep the Hungarians of Puskas and Hidegkuti to pre-eminence over the coming few years. It would culminate in the 3–6 humiliation of England, supposedly football's masters, at Wembley in 1953. While England followed the typically English virtues, as did around 95 per cent of our clubs, the Hungarians had taken football on to a new level, and Rowe was one of the few striving for it, too. Bill Shankly would ultimately adopt and adapt the technique into the Liverpool 'pass-and-move' philosophy that conquered Europe.

Writing a year after Reynolds' move in the Football Association's bulletin, Rowe attempted to put flesh on the bones of his tactical masterstroke.

'One of the slogans which partly describes our game is push and run, the application being to push the ball to a colleague and run into position for the immediate return pass. A simple progression on the favourite schoolboy trick of pushing the ball against a wall and moving forward to get the angled return beyond the opponent.

'Believing, too, that when a team loses possession of the ball it is often through their own bad play rather than their opponents' good play, we set great store on the "make it simple, make it accurate, and make it quick" slogan.

'Our goalkeeper as a last line of defence is also our first means of attack; our wing forwards as first lines of attack are very often key men in defence. We believe, in short, that when in possession, all players are attackers, and when not in possession, then all players are defenders.'

This utilitarian idea seemed incredible, almost Utopian, to the blinkered English establishment, which, as mentioned earlier, had long relied wholly on the 'WM' formation. With very few exceptions, just as people knew their place in society, so footballers knew their places on the field. An outside-right or outside-left would start just inside his own half and shuttle up and down the touchline. Inside-forwards would work what Ron Atkinson has subsequently termed 'the channels', though a few of the more gifted ones might receive a little licence to roam. Such liberalism didn't extend to the centre-forward, typically a brick shed of a footballer who would look to get on the end of crosses into the box from the wingers, the blunt instrument on the end of equally unsubtle attacking moves.

Rowe wanted to tear up those restrictive practices in a move that was wholly in keeping with the spirit of the age. All over the country people were trying to throw off the pre-war shackles that kept individualism suppressed. Post-war, people would no longer settle for being kept in the dark, given one specific, monotonous job to do day in, day out. Enlightened employers were beginning to trust their employees to do their jobs without the restriction of a ball and chain. The brightest were being given the opportunity to express themselves and perform in their own ways, often with exciting results.

Rowe felt that if he employed intelligent footballers – Alf Ramsey, Bill Nicholson, Ronnie Burgess – they needed only a few tactical guidelines rather than rigorous, mechanical strictures. Take out the mechanics from the game and create an organic, living, breathing, creative organism of a team rather than a plodding, predictable, if admittedly efficient, machine and you had a beast that could turn games inside out with just one spark, one moment of intuitive quality. Rowe delivered a freedom denied those playing under authoritarian managers who demanded that players did precisely what they were told.

That freedom certainly appealed to Ron, who still hankered after his days as an outfield player, and who felt that there was room for him in this vision of building your attacking moves from the back. Goalkeepers were forced to think quickly and release the ball fast in those days, lest they be clattered to the floor by a shoulder charge from an onrushing forward, so the opportunity to turn defence into the springboard for attack did exist when placed in the hands of an intelligent goalkeeper who could read the game well. By the end of his conversation with Anderson, Ron was sold on the move to Tottenham, particularly in light of the pay rise he was going to receive. Spurs were clearly overcome with feelings of generosity and, for his first season, rewarded Ron with the massive wage of just under £11 per week. His earnings would be catapulted into the stratosphere a year later when they shot up to £13 per week – enough money to turn anyone's head! The increased wages were important for a man who now had a young family to support. But he still refused to rely on football completely, diligently continuing with his studies as a hedge against the future. The improved pay would also offer some compensation for what would inevitably be immediate frustrations. Ron knew full well that by moving to north London he was exchanging an automatic first-team place in the Third Division South for a stretch in Tottenham's reserve side in the Football Combination. It was ever thus, and ever will be for the young goalkeeper, always looking to oust the senior player from just one place in the team. Ron accepted the situation with fortitude: 'When you play at one level of the game for some time, particularly at a lower level, then you do come to a point where you stop learning. If you are a younger player with ambitions, to let that situation continue is crazy. You really have to move to a higher level of the game if you want to progress, because you have to try to match yourself against better-quality players.

'Playing in the Third Division year in, year out, you come up against the same players, the same style of play and the same problems all the time and basically you stagnate because of that. I'd had three seasons where, injuries apart, I'd been a regular choice for Aldershot and I saw no point in having a fourth season doing the same things all over again. If I hadn't moved at that time, I'm sure my game would have deteriorated.

'And although the fact that goalkeepers go on longer can be a problem when you're a youngster, if you're fortunate with your health and with injuries, it does become a benefit at the other end of your career. Goalkeepers do improve with experience, and though you might not get into a top team until you're perhaps twenty-eight or twenty-nine, you can look forward to another ten years of football if you look after yourself. If you're an outfield player and you haven't made that step up to a big club at twenty-eight, then it's unlikely you ever will, because you might have only another four years left.'

The vital question was whether Spurs was too much of a step up in one go. Would Ron have been better served heading off to a Second Division side as a stepping-stone? If he'd done that, then first-team football was, if not guaranteed, at least highly probable.

'I did wonder if moving to Spurs to be Ted's deputy would be the right thing to do, but when you're young, you feel that you'll be able to show people how good you are very quickly. And with injuries much more commonplace among goalkeepers then, I did hope that as soon as I got one opportunity to play, I would be able to keep my place. Managers were more willing to give you a chance then, I think, and to persevere with you if you did well. If a big star was out with injury, he didn't automatically come back into the side if his replacement had done well.

'And you must remember that although I'd just turned twenty-two, I'd had quite a sheltered life to that point in that I was just a young lad from Haslemere. I'd lived there all my life, and had played all my football for a very small club in Aldershot. I was very keen to leave there in order to progress, and to improve my financial position, of course. So to have a club that had twice won the FA Cup and was back in the First Division chasing after you was very exciting. It would have been very difficult and probably foolhardy to turn them down.

'Because I was keen to learn, it didn't seem so much of a hardship to be understudy to Ted, either. He was an England goalkeeper, so who better to learn from than him, and from a manager like Arthur whom I admired greatly. I accepted that I might have to sit it out for a while, but that was my decision, and I didn't regret it, especially as the standard in the reserves was often much higher than it had been in Aldershot's first team.

'And playing in the reserves wasn't seen as such a chore as players seem to see it now. Of course, you didn't get the coverage that you did in the first team, you weren't in the limelight in that way, but we did get healthy crowds, bigger than Aldershot's in many cases! There was just more interest in every level and every aspect of a club then. It's hard to imagine that now when everything is focused purely on the first team. But then a manager took an interest in every team the club put out and so did the supporters. So it wasn't as if you were disappearing off the face of the earth. Arthur Rowe made you feel that everything anybody did while they were at Tottenham had a major bearing on the well-being of the club as a whole.'

That holistic approach to a football club is something that the game seems to have lost in recent years, with very few managers having any role beyond the preparation of the first team. That's as much a result of the new pressures of the industry as it is a question of choice. Managers are sacked on average every eighteen months these days, so you can't really blame them for not wanting to scratch beneath the surface. If they don't get results at first-team level, any work they do with the reserves or the youth team is going to help only their successors, not them. But Arthur Rowe really was the master of his domain, looking after every aspect of the club. It was an exhausting role, but one that perhaps brought greater fulfilment and a wider understanding of the club's wider needs, and those of the individuals who worked there.

Looking ahead to the 1950/51 season, Rowe felt that Spurs had a very good chance of making an impact on the First Division in their first attempt for fifteen years. Their relegation year, 1934/35, had seen Arsenal collect their third straight Football League title. It had not been much of a year to be in and around Seven Sisters. With his tactical outlook and a number of quality players on board, Rowe was sure that the gap between Second and First Division was far from insurmountable. And in those pre-TV-money days, there genuinely was little to choose between the bulk of First Division clubs and those in the upper reaches of the Second. Money flowed into the clubs almost wholly through the turnstiles, so if you could generate big crowds, you could compete financially with the likes of Arsenal and current champions Portsmouth, who had just won back-to-back titles. Furthermore, with players unable to move between clubs unless you wanted to sell them, retaining your best players was simple, enabling you to build a team that could threaten.

Tottenham's weakness was a lack of strength in depth, a problem that could be camouflaged in the Second Division but would be all too visible in more rarefied competition. That was the catalyst for the capture of Reynolds. Should Ditchburn be injured or away on international duty in those far-off days when the national side would often play its fixtures on the same day as a full set of league games, Spurs could now call on a goalkeeper of similar class to fill the breach. Teams rarely win anything without a top-class keeper, and even a few games under strength can mean the difference between success and failure.

The fact that Rowe had made the right choice was borne out almost immediately when his new goalkeeper made his first public appearance at the beginning of August 1950. Those were the days of public trial games, when a club's 'Probable' first eleven would come up against the 'Possibles' in a practice match. It was a fairly nerve-racking affair for the first-teamers, but a great opportunity for those, like Ron, who were waiting in the wings. Press reports were unanimously favourable: 'Spurs' Arthur Rowe has hit the jackpot again. A week or so ago he signed a young man from Aldershot who bore the label of "Best goalkeeper in the Third Division (South)". Ron Reynolds was the star of Tottenham's public trial. Keeping for the reserves, he was beaten five times, but stopped half a dozen shots from the Probables first team which had international Ted Ditchburn at the other end applauding.' Given the number of goals conceded, it was fortunate that Ron had had plenty of experience as

Ron pulls off a save for the 'Possibles' at White Hart Lane, 12th August 1950 (Empics)

a target in the coconut shy behind Aldershot's colander-like rear-guard. That alone must have helped him stay stoically unyielding in the face of such an onslaught. But even with such rave reviews, to be beaten so often was not exactly the start Ron was looking for. No wonder Ditchburn was applauding so enthusiastically.

CHAPTER SEVEN

December 1950 at White Hart Lane (Barratt's)

Although Ron enjoyed some success in that debut trial match for the Tottenham Possibles, there was never any doubt that he would begin his first season with them in the reserves. These were the days when there weren't any substitutes, never mind the whole phalanx of reserves occupying the dugout that we see today. Typically, if Tottenham's first team were playing host to Birmingham City one Saturday, then the reserves would be up in the Midlands taking on the Blues' second string at the same time. Logistically, this was simple enough since no reserves would need to be warming the bench at White Hart Lane. Ron certainly regarded it as a better situation than the one that exists today, which he described as 'Crazy! It seems that players are just put on the bench as a sop, because managers don't dare to drop them. And then they come on for ten or fifteen minutes. How can you get the pace of a game and then influence it in that space of time? It's a nonsense. Clubs carry far too many players these days, especially in the Premier League, and the substitutes' bench just seems to be a way of making sure they get a game and their appearance fees. I'm sure that's the only reason for some of the changes: to guarantee that a man gets his bonus.

'And it's devalued the reserve game, too. I know it's an old-fashioned view that football is for a Saturday afternoon, not even the first teams play then any more, but with no reserve games on the same day as first-team games because of this squad system nonsense, the reserves have to play at night in midweek, and that makes them much less attractive to supporters. It's one thing to go and watch them on Saturday afternoon – that's a tradition, or it was – but to make the effort to go out and watch reserve football in midweek is something else again.

'That's a great pity because it breaks one of the links between the supporters and the club. They did like to see the next generation of players in the second team, seeing who they thought would make the grade and who wouldn't. The fact that the crowds were there gave *you* extra incentive as a player, too. It helped if you got into the first team knowing that people in the crowd had seen you before, and knew what you could do. You felt more at ease, I suppose. It's a pity we don't have that any longer. Although you don't have reserves coming through into the first team so often, either: it's easier for managers to go and buy another player from abroad instead. That will ultimately cost us dear in this country.' Prophetic words in the light of England losing at home to Australia while under the charge of a Swedish manager.

Ron's attitude was never that he wished he'd had an easier life as a player, but rather that the current crop of footballers had a better grasp of how fortunate they are to be playing the game now. They can set themselves up financially, drive a sponsored, fully expensed car, and so on. The car especially was something Ron could have done with, given the journeys he'd let himself in for. Haslemere to White Hart Lane or, worse yet, to Tottenham's Cheshunt training ground was a pretty daunting daily trek, as Ron's son David remembers: 'When Dad was at Tottenham we didn't see a lot of him because he was commuting up there, so he'd drive up most days to Cheshunt, which was a hell of a drive for him to have to keep doing.

He used to tell me all these tales about the trouble he had getting to and from work, moaning about the roads. I was only four or five at the time but I remember the North Circular, Hanger Lane – the North Circular was pretty notorious in those days, probably even worse than it is now!'

Ron settled into his understudy role very quickly and was commended for his attention to training and for his performances in the reserves by Rowe, who was delighted that he had a youngster who would keep pushing Ditchburn to put in better performances. That level of competition was a crucial component in what soon turned out to be a remarkable season for Spurs, whose revolutionary brand of quick-moving, quick-thinking football left their more statuesque and prosaic rivals trailing in their wake, something which thrilled Ron whenever he had the chance to see the first team play.

'We did have a quite exceptional team at that time. I don't think I would say that we had lots of players that were head and shoulders above any others elsewhere in the country, though of course players like Alf Ramsey and Eddie Baily did get a number of England caps and had been involved in the World Cup in Brazil that summer. I think the difference between that Tottenham team and the others in the country was in the teamwork. Everyone really did play for the good of the team. There were no prima donnas in there, everyone did their bit and would cover for their team-mates.

'Most teams were quite predictable, but at Tottenham players had licence to do what they thought was right. So you'd get Alf, who was the right full-back, charging up over the halfway line and combining with his outside-right, which was unheard of in those days. Full-backs *never* went past halfway!

'That was the philosophy that Arthur instilled in the players: that you must always play for the good of the team, but if you saw an opportunity to create something, you shouldn't be afraid to go out of your position to do so, because you knew that someone would cover for you. It was about intelligence and movement, and Arthur encouraged that through the club, he encouraged us to talk about the game and to have new ideas. He wasn't frightened of his players, there was no insecurity, no paranoia about him, that he had to show he was the boss, as so many managers do. Arthur just wanted every-thing to improve and keep on improving. He was a remarkable manager, he really was.'

With his studies as a draughtsman completed, Ron was now free to concentrate entirely on his football, a chance he took with relish. He regularly stayed on after training was over to practise his skills further, and if he didn't have an extra session in mind, then he was only too happy to be sitting around with his team-mates, discussing the games ahead, any internationals that had taken place, or any other news doing the rounds on football's grapevine. David Reynolds recalls that 'Dad was always a listener when he felt he was with people who could teach him something, but he always liked to be able to have his say as well, so I think Tottenham under Arthur Rowe suited him down to the ground. In business, later on, he was a great believer in the idea of brainstorming and I'm sure that came from his time at Tottenham.'

As a genuine professional, in the best sense of that word, Ron was keen to use whatever spare time he had to improve as a player. Working on his practical skills was one element of that determination to improve, but, equally, his enquiring mind suggested that he should now gain a wider appreciation of the game as a whole. That feeling was enhanced by the company he kept: not only Arthur Rowe, but other players who were fascinated by the game in every respect, men like Bill Nicholson, Vic Buckingham and England amateur international George Robb, a teacher and coach at Ard-ingly School. At their prompting, Ron began to take an interest in coaching, as David recalls: 'I think he was very happy at Spurs, in terms of the sort of people running Tottenham, like the trainers and coaches and managers. He always spoke about Arthur Rowe and the new way of playing football that he thoroughly enjoyed, and that made him curious to do more. I think it was Arthur who got him on to the tack of doing his own coaching badge. Dad liked the thought of imparting his knowledge to others. He thought that if he were a qualified FA coach, then that might give him something to fall back on. He was always talking to other people about other opportunities just in case. He always had an eye on the fact that he would have to have another life once football finished. If you were earning only ten or fifteen pounds a week, you weren't going to make enough to retire on.' With his sensible, pragmatic approach to life, and his intense interest in every aspect of the game, it's likely that Ron would have eventually found himself following the coaching route, whichever club he'd joined. But there's no question that the environment at Tottenham accelerated that process, as he explained: 'I can't speak highly enough about Arthur Rowe in every sense, but especially as a theorist on the game. He felt that football was far too stereotyped in this country, that far too many teams played what we still have as the traditional English game, all about power and strength and running. Arthur had been abroad and seen the way continental teams approached football and he wanted to apply the things he had learned in Europe to the way we played at Tottenham, so that you could still have all the typical physical attributes but add a greater level of technique and tactical appreciation to that.

'Arthur, quite rightly, felt that coaching was the way to do that, not just as players but as people. At Cheshunt, we often spent as much time talking as we did practising. That was the way he did things. He accepted that as First Division players, you really ought to have mastered the basics of the game, but that was only the first step. He tried to make training sessions interesting and varied so that the players wouldn't become bored and treat them as a dull routine, so that they would get the maximum value from training, and he was very keen on physical fitness, too. But I suppose in comparison with today's players it all looks quite primitive, because plenty of the players still liked a smoke and a drink!'

David Reynolds remembers that in that respect his father stood out from the crowd because 'He hated smoking, he couldn't stand it! And he didn't drink much, so in that sense he looked after himself pretty well. But there was certainly no special diet that he followed as players do now. I know he never asked for any special food at home, just the same sort of things that everybody else ate. But those were the days when players would have a run round the streets surrounding the ground before sitting down to their pre-match meal a couple of hours before kick-off. They'd have a huge steak with chips, which wouldn't go down very well these days. I remember he always covered his food in salt, and that every morning he would religiously drink a tumbler of Andrews' Liver Salts, because he thought it cleared out the system.' Spurs may still have been in the Dark Ages regarding diet, but as Ron on a footballing level they were streets ahead, as Ron recalled: 'The really interesting thing about it all, which caught my attention the most, was that Arthur would talk to us about the game and would give us these little phrases to think about – "push and run", "make it simple, make it quick" – and these became the basis of our play. It was a change in the way people thought about the game and it opened my eyes as to what you could do with coaching. Before then, it just seemed to have been PT, very much as it might have been in the forces, just a lot of running around. But with Arthur, it went on in the mind, it was about creating spaces, angles, having ideas of your own within the set-up of the team. That was very interesting.

'As you would expect, Arthur had a lot of like-minded people around him. It ran through the club, including the players. I think the man most on his wavelength was Vic Buckingham, who went on to be a very good manager himself, at West Bromwich Albion and then in Europe. He was very involved with Ajax in the 1960s when they started to build that great team with Cruyff. Vic was just finishing his playing career when I joined Spurs, but he was very much in with the top coaches and instructors for the FA. I hadn't been there long when Vic, together with an Arsenal player of the day who was also an FA coach, Freddie Cox, held the very first course for a preliminary coaching certificate outside of the usual centres. That was held at Tottenham, so in Vic we had somebody who believed in football. But everybody at the club talked football.'

It was fortunate that Ron was bitten by the coaching bug so early in his days at Spurs, for it added an extra dimension to his life at the club. As anticipated, he sat out the whole of his first season at White Hart Lane. Ted Ditchburn stubbornly refused to give up his place in the team, turning in one impressive display after another as Tottenham made a startling return to the First Division. And that was after a catastrophic opener, beaten 1–4 at home by a Mortensen-and-

Matthews-inspired Blackpool, who had finished the previous season just four points away from the League Championship. Though the gulf in class looked immense, Rowe stuck to his tactical guns and by the end of August Spurs had earned a creditable 2–2 draw at Arsenal and two wins over Bolton, 4–2 at home and 1–4 away. September was patchy, but once they hit their stride Spurs were irresistible. October saw wins over Burnley, Stoke, West Bromwich Albion and Chelsea, but perhaps the most significant moment came in November, when the crown was passed as they slaughtered Portsmouth, champions in the previous two seasons, 7–1. Though Manchester United valiantly tried to keep pace with them, it was Tottenham's title from a long way out. They eventually finished four points clear of United, with third-place Blackpool a further six behind. Spurs' final total of sixty points was the highest amassed in twenty years.

With such a sparkling record, it's little wonder that there were few line-up changes throughout the season, and that Rowe kept things simple, the side all but selecting itself. From Ron's point of view, that

'Never change a winning team . . .' The Championship-winning side of 1951

was inevitably a double-edged sword: 'It was no surprise to me that I didn't play that season. That was the basis on which I signed for the club, and then when they did so well, I certainly didn't expect to get in. It doesn't hold true now, but then, the saying "Never change a winning team" was very much the rule.

'I did enjoy watching them play whenever I had the chance. They really were a joy to watch because they played such an exciting brand of football. It involved everyone in the side, from back to front, so that was particularly interesting for me to watch, because Ted Ditchburn wasn't only the last line of defence but also the first line of attack. That was very forward thinking.

'I think it was Ted, along with Bill Nicholson, who made Alf Ramsey such a good player for Spurs, to the point where he was the kingpin. It wasn't appreciated at the time, but now you've got those attacking wing-backs and I think Alf was one of the first to be doing this. As right full-back, Ramsey of course relied on Nicholson a hell of a lot. He was able to go up and support Willis, who played as the outside-right, and Nicholson just slotted back. He was a dour player, Bill Nicholson, and he just suited Ramsey's game.

'In my opinion Arthur Rowe had perfected the push-and-run style, and this suited Alf perfectly. You would see Alf running back towards his own goal, the ball in front of him and he used to delay a ball back to Ted Ditchburn. He did that to give the winger who was chasing the opportunity or the thought that he could get it. And then of course Alf used to peel off towards the touchline and Ted just threw it to him. This was fascinating for me to watch because it was something I'd never seen at Aldershot. And then Alf used to bypass Nicholson, to Sonny Walters.

'Sonny was very fleet of foot, a very fast winger. If he got a ball, he went like lightning. But at the same time there were individuals who were even more important. Ronnie Burgess: the way he used to bring Eddie Baily and Les Bennett in to play was brilliant. Les was up front alongside Len Duquemin; Eddie was the fleet-of-foot player behind him. I would say that Ronnie Burgess was a human dynamo. He probably got through more work than even Danny Blanchflower did when he joined us a few years later, and that's saying something.'

For all that Ron was in a privileged position to soak up the intelligence and imagination of what was going on around him, he didn't deny that there were frustrations arising from his position in the reserves.

'I'll pay tribute to Arthur again, because he did make all of us feel that we were playing our part in the club's success. He believed that if you had a strong reserve team, you would have a strong first team and he was right. We were all encouraged to play well in the reserves to keep the first-teamers on their toes, though I don't think he allowed the reserves to come through into the first team quickly enough.

'Although reserves changed in a different dressing room to the first-team players, he always wanted us to talk football, and that made us feel that we were participating in the improvement of the team and the club, that we all had something to say and that we would be listened to. But if you're not taking part in the games, then I don't think you ever feel fully a part of what is happening: there is always some detachment from it. I've spoken to players who have been in a similar position with their club, and even men who have been in England squads, and they always say the same. If you don't play, you don't feel fully involved.

'I don't want to be churlish about it because it was a wonderful thing to be involved with the club at that time. I learned a great deal that first season, and it was that which led me into learning about coaching, which I became very enthusiastic about. But by the end of that season, I was itching to play for the first team.'

Unfortunately for Ron, that itch would persist for quite some time to come.

CHAPTER EIGHT

The White Hart Lane training regime

Ron Reynolds might have felt like something of a spare part when it came to the side that took the title, but Spurs made every effort to ensure that he and all the other reserves enjoyed some of the spoils of victory. As was mentioned, wages went up, and there were the inevitable celebrations to follow. A special dinner was held in honour of the club at London's Café Royal: pretty swanky surroundings for a goalkeeper who still saw himself as just 'a young, wide-eyed country lad from Haslemere'.

Recalling that night forty-five years later, Ron had some vivid memories of the occasion: 'I did feel a bit overawed by it all. I felt out of place, if you like. I was from a small country town, I'd played most of my football in the Third Division, and suddenly I was off to the Café Royal, which was the centre of London society. I was still getting used to the fact that I was with Tottenham and that I worked with all those big-name internationals, but this was something else entirely, and I felt awkward leading up to the night because I'd had just one season there. And that was in the reserves.

'My wife didn't come with me – she had absolutely no interest in football at all or any of the social life that went with it – so I went on my own. It was a very enjoyable evening in many ways: we had a very nice meal, and then there was dancing.

'Alf Ramsey came up to me and said, "I want you to meet somebody." He introduced me to his wife and within thirty seconds said, "You won't mind having a dance with her, will you?" He didn't want to dance and I'd been lumbered! She was a very nice person, but that was the only occasion I ever spoke to her. And I was practically speechless then!'

The 1951/52 season was not as memorable for Ron. 'I was delighted to be at a club where we'd won the League Championship so convincingly and played so much exciting football. It was a privilege to be part of such a thing and I was very conscious of that fact. But it did come with its own particular disadvantages. Returning for the new season, I was very aware that there was no more realistic chance of my getting into the first team than there had been the year before, and I found that a little upsetting, though it was quite understandable – I wouldn't have expected anything else. Ted Ditchburn was still good enough to be involved with the England team at times, and he was a championship-winning goalkeeper who wasn't yet old enough to be thinking of retirement, so it was inevitable that he would be in goal.

'My approach was as it had been the previous year: to continue learning about goalkeeping in training, by listening to Arthur and the coaching staff and by watching Ted. I was still quite young, so it hadn't reached a serious point at that stage, but obviously I was keen to start playing first-team football again. Probably there were twenty-one other reserve-team goalkeepers in the First Division who felt very much the same way.'

Ron's hopes of breaking into the first team were not helped by the fact that Tottenham pretty much picked up from where they had left off the previous season, retaining the basic principles of the push-and-run game and playing with the same level of verve and invention that had carried them to the title. They lacked the element of surprise that had been a key weapon the previous season, but the confidence in their own abilities was such that that was of less consequence. Even when they were on the receiving end of the occasional thumping, such as a 7–2 defeat against Newcastle United early in the season, their belief in what they were doing and the way in which they were doing it meant they were almost anaesthetised to the shocks . . . And while Tottenham's style wasn't quite the surprise package it had been, push and run still had great novelty value, simply because football was not analysed and picked to pieces in the way it is now. These were days long before televised football, before *Match of the Day* and the panel of pundits. Though you might have seen push and run, you'd only encounter it on the couple of occasions each season when you were up against Spurs. So the opposition were hard pressed to come up with a viable means of stopping it. Ron certainly knew that his Spurs side benefited by playing in the pre-television era: 'The TV and media now is so widespread that all of the good things and all of the bad things are emphasised over and over again. Tactically, if you have a particularly clever free-kick routine or something of that nature, you can try it out only once and hope it works, because once that game is over everyone will get to see it before you've played again, and they'll be watching for it. I think this is why you find that so many teams lack imagination at free-kicks now. They either go for the brute force of trying to belt the ball through the wall or, if they're fortunate, they have someone like Cantona or Beckham who tries to score direct. When they take a free-kick, we all know what it is they're going to try to do; it's just a question of whether they succeed or not. It's a great ability that they have, but I'd like to see some more imaginative free-kicks sometimes.

'The unfortunate thing with the media is that the bad things stick, but the good things don't necessarily. This has always been the same, whether you see a game on TV or at the ground. I can remember as a youngster going to watch teams on the local rec. where I lived, and seeing a player from one of the local sides back-heel a ball as a pass! In the weeks to follow at school we were all doing the same thing.

'It can be more serious, of course, when you have bad behaviour: the gesturing, the swearing. Children see that, see there is no sanction, and then copy it. And the media glorifies it. So the media have got a lot to answer for. It's great to be able to pinpoint the good things, but the bad things that show up are even more important.'

Ron was always a stickler for correct behaviour, as his son David points out: 'Another of his pet subjects was that you never questioned the authority of the referee or the linesman. Whether you agreed with them or not, they were always right and their word was sacrosanct and you simply got on with it. He was an argumentative so-and-so off the field at times and he would always want to have his say, but when he was playing, he always used to say that the referee's word was final.' That view is reinforced by Brian Pearce, games master at Lanesborough Preparatory School in Guildford from 1949 to 1988, and a lifelong friend of Ron's.

'I came to know Ron through coaching because when Walter

Waiting for a first-team opportunity at White Hart Lane, March 1951

Winterbottom was the director of coaching at the Football Association, he had a scheme where selected schools would receive a certain amount of free coaching from one of the advanced coaches at the FA. I was at Lanesborough and Ron came down for the Christmas term in 1954. After that he came regularly until 1963.'

'Ron was very well informed on the laws of the game, which is not something you could say about most footballers, then or now. Like Ron, my main interest was coaching and I went up to Loughborough for a two-week course in 1954 for the FA coaching certificate. The only person to get the advanced certificate was Alan Wade, who ultimately replaced Walter Winterbottom as the head of coaching at the FA. Walter was a man before his time, a sort of Arsène Wenger, an academic who didn't get flustered or shout the odds but put the message across in a calm, cool way. Walter was a superb lecturer on coaching and on the laws of the game. I went back in 1955 when Norman Creek was in charge, but I had a back injury and couldn't get involved in the games, so I sat and did some analysis – shots on target, accuracy of passes, number of passes – and then went through it afterwards. For one game, I was asked to referee, which I'd never done before. After the game, Norman came striding over to me and insisted that I go on home and become a referee. I qualified in January 1956. A lot of that was due to Ron and conversations with him about points of law because he was extremely knowledgeable, informative and encouraging. I felt he played a big part in my becoming a referee. He discussed many things with me, especially with regard to the goal area, where goalkeepers had a little extra protection.'

Those coaching activities were still in the future for Ron. He saw the current season as a time to focus on his own development as a player: 'I did become a better goalkeeper perhaps more because of that second season than the first at Tottenham. I think when young players move from a very small club to a very big one – and you can't get any bigger than the team that wins the league, can you? – it takes them a while to settle in there. I was surrounded by people like Ditchburn and Ramsey, great names in the game, you saw them in the newspapers and the football magazines, and yet I was training with them. It is a big transition to make and I think many players would say that, for the first few months, they feel out of place in those circumstances.

'If you aren't settled in your surroundings, then there's no way you can play at your best and for most of the first season in the reserves I felt under some pressure just to show people how good I was. And I was also coming to terms with playing at a level that was generally higher than the standard in the Third Division, even though it was reserve football. On top of that, it was new for me to be travelling so far to get into training every day. I wasn't really totally comfortable until the end of the 1950/51 season, so it was nice to return the following season knowing that Arthur Rowe was pleased with my progress, knowing I could just concentrate on my game rather than settling in.'

It was also nice to know that the goalkeepers' union was working to good effect. Press reports of the time noted, 'Ditchburn and Reynolds are both very fine fellows and the very firmest of friends. Each helps the other wherever possible and is delighted with his colleague's successes. There is not a hint of jealousy between them and they can often be found yarning about the game long after training is over for the day.'

If Ron's career was helped by Ditchburn's advice, so the senior keeper's performances were enhanced by having the younger man breathing down his neck. Ditchburn certainly maintained the high standards he had set for himself as Spurs looked to follow Portsmouth's post-war example and retain their title. The competition was stiffer this time, and Spurs' general play not quite up to the standard of the previous season. They appeared to suffer from the post-title fatigue that afflicts many sides who have scaled the mountain only to find they have to start from the bottom all over again a few months later. To their credit, a virtually unchanged set of players kept things ticking over at White Hart Lane, and they remained in the title hunt throughout another long, hard season. But the winter months hit them hard, as push and run was bogged down on heavier pitches than had been encountered the year before. By the end of a poor December, they were four points adrift of Manchester United. Then they were dumped unceremoniously out of the FA Cup by holders Newcastle United, who won 0–3 at White Hart Lane. Spurs managed to stay on Manchester United's coat-tails into the final stretch, but Busby's team maintained their four-point cushion until the end. Spurs settled for the runners-up spot.

The most telling statistic in an ultimately disappointing season was that United won the title with three points fewer than Spurs had amassed the year before. Over the twelve months, Tottenham had shed seven points: powerful evidence that they were a team in decline. Having also conceded seven more goals in the season, was there finally a chink of light for a reserve goalkeeper who'd had another solid, if unspectacular, season in the Football Combination?

Date	Opponents	Ground	Result			Date	Opponents	Ground	Result		
			WON LEAGUE BY 1 Pt. FROM PORTSMOUTH						TOTTENHAM 39 PTS 24 GAMES 71-32 2.213 A PORTSMOUTH 38 PTS 27 GAMES 63-31 2.09 A		
1952						**Dec.-Cont**					
Aug. 23	Cardiff City 8,000	Away	0	1	L.	" 27	Coventry City 2,000	Home	3	3	D
" 25	West Ham United 6,000	Away	2	2	D.	**1953**					
" 30	Arsenal 15,000	Home	1	1	D.	Jan. 3	Arsenal 7,000	Away	2	0	W.
Sept. 6	Reading 4,000	Away	1	2	L.	" 10	Fulham 5,000	Away	4	1	W
" 8	Birmingham City 4,000	Home	5	2	W.	" 17	Reading 7,000	Home	5	1	W
" 13	Southampton 7,000	Home	2	1	W.	" 24	Southampton 7,000	Away	0	2	L.
" 20	Millwall 8,000	Away	0	0	D.	May 2	Millwall 2,000	Home	2	1	W
" 22	West Ham United 4,000	Home	3	0	W.	Undated	Birmingham City	Home	2	0	W.
" 27	Cardiff City 500	Away	1	1	D.		COMBINATION CUP				
" 29	Coventry City 5,500	Away	2	2	D.	Jan. 31	Brentford 2,000	Away	1	0	W.
Oct. 4	Portsmouth 6,000	Away	0	1	L.	Feb. 7	Queen's Park Rangers	Home	1	0	W.
" 6	Norwich City 4,000	Home	1	0	W.	" 14	Brentford 5,000	Home	3	0	W.
" 11	Charlton Athletic 8,000	Home	3	0	W.	" 21	Queen's Park Rangers	Away	2	1	W
" 13	Plymouth Argyle	Home	5	1	W.	" 28	Brighton & Hove	Home	1	1	D.
" 18	Northampton Town	Away	1	0	W.	Mar. 7	Brighton & Hove	Away	2	0	W.
Nov. 8	Fulham 8,000	Home	0	0	D.	" 14	Crystal Palace 3,000	Away	0	1	L.
" 15	Charlton Athletic 2,000	Away	9	1	W.	" 21	Chelsea 5,000	Home	1	1	D.
" 22	Plymouth Argyle 7,500	Away	2	3	L.	" 28	Chelsea 3,000	Away	5	0	W.
Dec. 6	Northampton Town 2,000	Home	2	2	D.	Apr. 4	Crystal Palace 4,000	Home	3	2	W
" 13	Chelsea 6,000	Away	4	1	W.	" 6	Southend United 5,000	Away	4	2	W
" 20	Portsmouth 7,000	Home	1	1	D.	" 8	Southend United 2,000	Home	3	2	W
" 25	Norwich City 5,000	Away	2	2	D.	" 18	Arsenal 18,000	Home	0	2	L

PENALTY SCORED - FOR. 10
PENALTY SCORED - AGAINST. +
PENALTY MISSED OR SAVED
PENALTY SAVED * 11
PENALTY MISSED BY OPP.

Ron Reynolds' annotated account of the
1952–53 reserve team season

For the outsider or the dispassionate observer, understanding the dynamics of a football team can be difficult. For most of us, in normal office or factory jobs, once we have proven that we can fulfil a specific role, that's pretty much it. The job is done ad infinitum, because if you're working on a lathe or in an accounts office, age has little impact on your ability to do the job. You have your good days and your bad days, but generally they even out in the long run. A working team can therefore be together for a prolonged period, with people leaving mainly when they want to go, rather than being forced out of their job. For the professional footballer, that's not the case. Nowadays, it's a little harder to find much sympathy for them and their insecure profession, given the telephone-number salaries that some can command, but whatever the level of pay, the same bottom line remains: once you've reached your peak, there's only one way to go. Age is the great enemy of all professional sportsmen and women, and it's an enemy you will never beat. The greatest truism in the game is that a footballer eventually reaches a point where he can no longer physically perform to the level that he once did. Then he has only two options: move down the league ladder or hang up the boots for good.

It's often easier for the supporters on the terraces or the journalists in the press box to spot a player's decline than it is for those right in the midst of things. If a player is having a rough time, his teammates will do their best to cover for him. Football dressing rooms are very tightly knit, almost tribal in their intensity, so if one of their number is wounded, they can be fierce in their protection of him, especially if things are going relatively well on the field. Footballers, as a breed, seem to abhor change, perhaps seeing a precursor of their own eventual demise in that of a colleague. After all, who wants to be reminded of their own mortality, their own eventual retirement and, in the days when Ron was playing, a departure back into the 'real world' and the necessities of making an 'ordinary' living? Perhaps it's because players wear numbers that they seem somehow impersonal to the fans, inhuman almost. In *The Prisoner* Patrick McGoohan might have complained that he was not a number, but, sadly, that's very much how we view players, even those who are fans' favourites. In the final analysis, to the supporters, a goalkeeper is only the bloke who wears number 1 on his back (or maybe number 42 these days). And once he's showing signs of flagging, of not living up to the job in hand, then he gets pretty short shrift from the spectators, who are focused only on the final result rather than the destiny of the man. In the inner sanctum of the dressing room it's very different. Imagine that the person who occupies the desk next to yours is suddenly pensioned off or sacked. How would you and the rest of the office take to that? How easy would it be for you, in a position of authority, to do the sacking yourself, to tell that individual that they're past it and that you're bringing in some new blood to take over? Looked at from the human point of view rather than from the sporting angle, the whole process takes on a very different aspect, doesn't it?

But that is what we all expect our football clubs and our football managers to do on a regular basis: not just at the end of a season, but during it, almost on a weekly basis if the side is flagging. The 'gaffer' is expected to sacrifice a player who might have given his all to him and to the club for five or ten seasons and throw him out on his ear just to rejuvenate the team. Of course, that's a central part of the job and one of the biggest reasons why it is so tough. The manager plays God with the lives of his players, which must be incredibly stressful, even for the most self-absorbed and hard-nosed individuals. To tell someone of perhaps limited means – especially in the 1950s – that they're on the scrap heap and need to start thinking about opening a tobacconist's shop somewhere must take its toll.

And in a sporting environment, there's the added factor that the players live on top of one another throughout the season. If a team like Spurs were playing in Newcastle, for example, it'd mean an all-day journey by train or coach in one another's company, followed by an overnight stay before the game, maybe even one afterwards, and then another massive cross-country trek home. It's hardly surprising that intense, if paradoxically ephemeral, friendships develop: many players of that era refer to their time together as akin to membership of a brotherhood. Unsurprising too that managers looked on players who had done great things for them almost as surrogate children. Who would be in any great hurry to throw out beloved family members on the grounds of diminished performance alone?

That is probably the greatest challenge that has to be faced by football managers, and perhaps the single biggest reason why even the most successful rarely have a tenure at a club that extends beyond the construction of one great side: that which you have built you're loath to destroy. Even the greats have wrestled with the problem. Bill Shankly took Liverpool through a comparative trough in the late 1960s when he hung on to the likes of Hunt, Thompson and Lawrence for too long before belatedly refreshing his side with Heighway, Keegan and Clemence. He then left the job before he was forced to tear down a second great side and deal with the anguish it caused him. He knew he simply couldn't bear to part with players he loved and who had done so much for him. Though Matt Busby built three great sides, the creation of the third was enforced by the Munich tragedy, and then he was also caught out in the end.

Too many members of the 1968 European Cup-winning side stayed in place after they had exhausted their useful working lives. But who could blame Busby for the emotional bond he had with the likes of Bobby Charlton after all they'd been through together? More recently, the legendary Arsenal defence, first created in what seems like the Stone Age, were left to get old together by Arsène Wenger, condemning Arsenal to a trophyless spell. Even Alf Ramsey, often portrayed as the least sentimental of men, held on to too many of his England internationals for too long, that decision finally costing him his own job. Only Alex Ferguson seems to have the ruthlessness required to deconstruct teams almost as soon as they hit their peak, to replace them with fitter, hungrier, leaner individuals.

In 1951/52, Tottenham had started well enough before the mid-season slump in December saw them fall behind Manchester United. The fact that they recovered to chase the Reds all the way to the line suggested that this might simply have been a blip, especially as they still finished second and, crucially, above Arsenal. A more accurate reading of the runes, however, would have shown that the December slump, which saw Spurs beaten at home by Liverpool and Charlton Athletic and away by Blackpool and West Bromwich Albion – none of whom finished in the top eight – was a symptom of a deeper malaise. Not only had the physical edge been dulled, but there seemed to be players in the side who could no longer raise their games for the more mundane fixtures. Surely now was the time for changes.

But Spurs entered 1952/53 much as they had left 1951/52, to the great disappointment of Ron and several of his reserve-team colleagues. 'I think that ultimately it wasn't that we lost the value of the tactics of push and run. I think that, as a way of playing, it could have carried on successfully for many years, as it did in many ways, I suppose, for different clubs later on. The way Liverpool played was very much in that style, even Manchester United when they finally started to win things again with Alex Ferguson. Good football is all about movement and intelligence, and that hasn't changed. If people do things quickly and accurately against you, there's not much you can do to stop them.

Still in training, August 1952 (Barratt's)

'So I don't think they were rumbled as much as that, Arthur delayed for too long before bringing in the players that he had at his disposal. He had such players as Tommy Harmer, Sid McClellan, Tommy Dyson that he could have brought in much earlier than he did. It was a long time before he brought in Peter Baker and Ronnie Henry, who were doing great things in the reserves and who did eventually show their value in the first team. I think it was that more than anything that saw Spurs decline for a while.

'The team stood still – actually, it was decaying – while others such as Manchester United, Wolves, West Brom, were getting stronger, and that was a great pity. People have tried to suggest that the club didn't have reserves of sufficient quality, but I think that's crazy. I played with these people and I know how good they were. Even if they hadn't been, Tottenham were a very big club, they had money, they could have brought in new players. No, the simple truth was that Arthur Rowe was so attached to the players who had won promotion and then the championship for him that he simply didn't want to part with them. And that was Arthur's only failing as a manager. But what a strength it was for him as a man.'

History shows that Rowe clearly got it wrong, and that Tottenham would not go on to dominate the 1950s as they might have done. Instead, the team slowly petered out. The 1952/53 season was a deep disappointment to all their followers, as the league campaign was all but over in the first three months as they languished in lower mid-table. In traditional Tottenham fashion, the depression caused by their league form was cast aside at the turn of the year for a thrilling FA Cup run that started with the trouncing of Tranmere, 9–1, in a third-round replay. Then they beat Tom Finney's Preston in another replay, then Halifax Town and Birmingham City in yet another replay on their way to the semi-final at Villa Park. Unfortunately, there they came across Blackpool and, in particular, Stanley Matthews on his way to his destiny at Wembley and the legendary 1953 FA Cup Final. Tottenham went down 2–1, a mishit Ramsey back pass in the dying seconds putting Jackie Mudie in on goal to slip a shot past Ditchburn.

For Reynolds, the loss of even a little glamour by association and a trip as reserve to the Cup Final pretty much summed up the year he'd had, when he played solidly in the second team, but still got no closer to dispossessing Ditchburn. In an era when goalkeepers should have been on danger money, so numerous were the injuries they sustained, Ditchburn was barely scratched. He was amassing an extraordinary run of consecutive appearances for Spurs, the run not even interrupted by international call-ups, since his England days were now behind him.

Three years of waiting patiently in the wings was becoming too much, and Ron admitted that he wondered if his game might be suffering: 'I felt much as I did in my last year at Aldershot: that I had done another part of my apprenticeship. I felt that it really was time that I got some opportunities in the first team. And that's in no way to suggest that Ted wasn't still a very, very good goalkeeper and worthy of his place in the team. But, like any player who feels he has anything to offer, I didn't want to spend all my time in the reserves. Even when I was there, there were still some who suggested that I might be a possible England international in the future. While I didn't pay too much attention to what people said about me in that regard, I began to feel that I should at least get an opportunity in the first team.

'I certainly had no desire to leave Tottenham and I fully understood Arthur's need to have an experienced understudy at the club, but I can't say I was entirely happy. At the same time, there weren't many better clubs to play for than Spurs. We were one of the biggest in the country, and most steps would have been backwards from there. I wanted to keep moving forward. I was settled where I was, I had a family, and these were important considerations.

'And, of course, I did enjoy working with Arthur and the rest of the people at Tottenham. The main thing was that, although there were frustrations − of course there were − I didn't feel that I had stopped learning. It was a very fertile ground for ideas about football: there were a lot of very good men there who were interested in the way the game should go, and I caught the coaching bug from them.

'That made life interesting for me, and I was a regular on the FA coaching courses and started doing additional work as a coach myself. I found this absolutely fascinating and, because I could fully throw myself into this work, it may have eased the frustrations I felt from not making more progress at Spurs.'

It may also have eased any financial frustrations brought about by his inability to get hold of any of those first-team bonuses that sometimes flew about. Ron's tax returns for the year to April 1953 show that his income from Tottenham was £714 10s – around £13 15s per week. But Ron augmented that with further coaching income that reached £153 6s, a nice little bonus that certainly made life more palatable for him. However, the financial benefit wasn't his only concern: 'It was a very exciting period as far as coaching went because that was when it first really started to take off in this country, in the years just after the war. Walter Winterbottom is always thought of as the first England manager, but that was only a very small part of what he did, and what his position was with the Football Association. His main role, and certainly his most important role to my mind, was as the director of coaching. He transformed the way people thought of coaching in this country.

'There were still many many clubs where there was little or no tactical appreciation, and where even the basics of the game were completely ignored. Even into the 1950s, at so many clubs, all they did in training was run cross-country or throw medicine balls at one another in the gym. Of course, physical fitness is vitally important if you are an athlete, but there was this absurd idea that if you didn't see a football in training from Monday to Friday, then you'd be desperate to get hold of it on a Saturday. These were people who had been in football all their lives coming up with these ideas, and it was just crazy. Arthur Rowe always felt that if you hadn't seen the ball all week, then you wouldn't recognise it on Saturday, and he was right.

'But Walter was the man who really made coaching acceptable. He made it something you had to know about if you wanted to understand the game. I found the whole thing absorbing, utterly fascinating and I felt lucky to be a part of what was the first coaching movement in this country.'

The importance of coaching, and just how far we lagged behind the world, would be demonstrated in the most brutal way possible early on in the coming 1953/54 season when the Mighty Magyars descended upon Wembley Stadium and blew away England's myth of invincibility in a flurry of goals.

But as preparations for that season got under way, it was still touch and go as to whether the extracurricular thrill of coaching would be enough to keep Reynolds in the Lilywhites' fold, especially as another First Division team was desperate to prise him away from White Hart Lane.

CHAPTER TEN

In only his second League match Ron pulls off a string of saves at
Stamford Bridge, 27th March 1954 (A Ronald Traube)

The English summer of 1953 went down as one of the more memorable of the twentieth century, certainly in peacetime. It started with Stanley Matthews, the wizard of the dribble, inspiring Blackpool to come back from 1–3 down to clinch the FA Cup with a 4–3 win over Bolton Wanderers. For the first time, Britons in substantial numbers beyond the 100,000 crammed into Wembley Stadium were able to watch the game unfold on jerky black-and-white TV pictures as the box started to find its way into British front parlours, in good time for the second key event of the summer: the coronation of Queen Elizabeth II. That may well have been the single most significant event in the growth of TV in this country, as people scrimped and saved to buy a TV. It may even have been the start of the credit boom, as people began to buy goods on the 'never never'.

Vastly removed from the indifference that attended the monarch's Golden Jubilee, or even the Pistolian bile that pogoed around the periphery of the Silver Jubilee, Coronation year saw a huge out-pouring of patriotism in what was still a fervently royalist country. But the coronation also marked a new beginning, a final shaking off of the horrors of war and the post-war austerity that followed. We were new Elizabethans and, symbolically at least, we were heading into a new, bright era.

As if to confirm that, England regained the Ashes from Australia for the first time in nineteen years, the series win built on the old-fashioned persistence of Trevor Bailey and Willie Watson, whose stonewalling saved the Lord's Test. Then up stepped the swashbuck-ling Compton and Edrich to complete the series win, both at the crease as the winning runs were clubbed at The Oval.

But the sporting honeymoon and all its promise were short lived. For in 1953 the Hungarians dismantled England at Wembley, winning 3–6 at a canter. Ron Reynolds wasn't completely surprised by the defeat: 'We didn't know how good the Hungarians really were in this country, because we didn't get to see international foot-ball from abroad as easily as you can nowadays on Sky. The most you might ever see would be a clip on a newsreel at the cinema. But we did know that the Hungarians were getting wonderful results, because the football magazines reported that quite well. And from my visits to Lilleshall, I could see that many English clubs were so antiquated in what they were doing. At Tottenham, Arthur had revo-lutionised the English game with push and run and we'd shown that if you could play it well, teams just could not cope with it. I spent many of my summers at Lilleshall with the Football Association's coaching programmes, and some of the ideas about coaching, about tactics and about training were light-years away from what most clubs were doing.

'I always felt that if we knew about these systems, then they must know about them abroad. Indeed, many of the things that the coaches were talking about were ideas they'd brought back after staying with clubs in Italy or Germany or Hungary and observing what they did. Watching the football that most clubs up and down the country played, which was still based on strength and power and what we now call the long-ball game, it was obvious we were still in the Dark Ages. Wolves were the most obvious example of that: there wasn't much finesse about them, just a lot of hard running which was enough to win trophies in those days. And, to be fair, they did it superbly well.'

Ron's comments were echoed in the Football Association's own bulletin in 1955, when Ivan Sharpe paid fulsome tribute to Alf Ramsey, then newly retired as a player. Terming him 'the man who showed the way', Sharpe wrote, 'Ramsey is one of the players we shall miss and are unlikely, soon, to replace. It was the same with Wilf Mannion and Peter Doherty at inside-forward.

'We do not replace them because of the atmosphere of hurry and scurry and desperation in which our league games are now played. Until this tension is eased – the excessive importance of points; the orgy of spoiling, destructive play; the frenzy in what passes in 1955 for first-class league football – few Ramseys, Mannions and Dohertys will arise to grace the game and play first-class football, because the arts and crafts are being shrivelled in the furnace.

'Ramsey reminded everyone that a full-back's job, like that of a half-back, is only half done when he has secured possession of the ball. No, NOT half. Surely it isn't so difficult to place a pass with the side of the foot from full-back. Surely many more young men can do it if their clubs will encourage them. Surely the average Football League full-back knows in his heart that a clearance lashed or driven far up the field is often of no value whatever to his colleagues. Why then does he do it?

'Tension. Frenzy. The excessive importance of points.'

In a further article in the same bulletin, portentously entitled 'Our Game – Today & Tomorrow by The Players' Union', similar thoughts were expressed, though, this time, much of the criticism was aimed at the great unwashed who filed through the turnstiles: 'It would help a great deal if, through the medium of Club Programmes or even the local Press, the education of spectators in the good and bad tactics of the game could be promoted. Even now, after all the publicity given to the accurate passing of the Continental sides, many still cheer the big kick up field, whilst the accurate short pass is often groaned at.'

Both the players' spokesman and Sharpe could have written virtually the same account in any season, up to and including this one, and it was a sentiment with which Reynolds wholly concurred. But at least, for him, there was a saving grace. 'I was fortunate being at Spurs because we were a progressive football club in that regard, and it was always interesting to hear just what everyone had to say. But as a country, I thought we were very old fashioned, and that was shown up by our failures in the European Cup until 1968. Though perhaps the Busby Babes might have succeeded before then because Matt Busby was very forward looking, in the same mould as Arthur Rowe.'

Ron certainly was fortunate that the way in which the Spurs players talked about the game held his interest, because he was still looking at life from the sidelines as the 1953/54 season kicked off, with Spurs continuing with a similar side to the one that had won the League Championship three seasons before.

In spite of his inactivity at first-team level, Ron's reputation within the game had continued to grow as he maintained the highest standards in the reserves. Rowe recognised his qualities and tried to give him every opportunity in the first team in friendlies or other low-key games, such as the Coronation Cup, a competition which pitted English teams against their Scottish counterparts in May 1953. The press described him as 'uncannily brilliant' against Hibernian. The praise continued into the summer as Spurs headed off to Shottermill, Ron's home town, for a friendly benefit game. The local newspaper, naturally predisposed to Ron anyway, wrote, 'Lesson number one was "Goalkeeping made easy" and it was given by Ron Reynolds, who lives at Shottermill and who is pretty obviously Ditchburn's successor in the Spurs goal. Reynolds, who has improved beyond all knowledge since his Aldershot days, gave an impeccable display of nonchalant goalkeeping. More, he made attack after attack by his judicious clearances, always to an unmarked player. One shot looked hopeful, but Reynolds plucked it from mid-air with the ease of a boy picking apples.'

Having Spurs descend on Shottermill was certainly a gala occasion, as Arthur Masey, himself a semi-pro player with Leatherhead, recalls: 'Ron brought a team down from Spurs because one of the local boys had a bad accident, and I was asked to turn out for Shottermill. It was very nice of them to do that. It wasn't the full team of course, mainly youngsters, but Ron played and it was a big day for everyone. The benefit game was a wider success, raising nearly £90 in a variety of ways according to the report. 'Gate receipts were £65 10s. 3d. and £11 12s. 9d. resulted from the sale of programmes. A basket of fruit given by Mr. R. Marshall raised £11 18s. 9d. Expenses amounted to £11 9s including printing and the cost of refreshments. A notable gesture was that of Liphook Football Club who supplied the shirts and socks for the match free of charge.'

Further evidence that Ron remained an important member of the local community comes from Masey who recalls, 'We played a bit of cricket together for Shottermill End after the war: he was a decent local standard, useful batsman, very orthodox and a pretty handy wicket-keeper as well, as you'd probably expect.'

Ron's consistent, high-quality displays, at whatever level, were always going to keep him uppermost in the minds of those inside the game who were 'in the know'. It was only a matter of time before other clubs began to believe they could persuade Spurs to release him and give him a chance of regular first-team football elsewhere. The first to try their luck were Portsmouth, in September 1953, as they sought a replacement for their injured goalkeeper, Norman Uprichard. According to press reports of the time, 'Arthur Rowe, Spurs' manager, regards Reynolds as a model player both on and off the field, and would like to see him enjoying the limelight he deserves. But Reynolds is the only reserve keeper at White Hart Lane with sufficient experience at present to deputise for Ditchburn, and for this reason Manager Rowe was forced to give Portsmouth a negative answer.

'"If I had another experienced reserve, I would have considered the Portsmouth offer, but as things are I could not expose my club to such a risk," Arthur tells us. The move would have suited Reynolds, whose home is at Haslemere, close to Portsmouth "country". But Ron's reaction was typical of him. "I'd love to play for Portsmouth," he told Manager Rowe, "but I appreciate your position, and am ready to accept it in Tottenham's interests."'

All very civilised, though Ron later admitted that even back in the 1950s the press were prone to putting a bit of spin on matters: 'In situations such as those, as a player you had no choice in the matter. The transfer had been proposed and rejected long before I heard anything about it. As a player, the clubs felt it was nothing to do with you at all! That was why there were few managers who you ever felt any admiration for, but Arthur was one of those because he had all the feelings of a player, he knew what you felt about situations that came up.

'Apart from Aldershot, Pompey were the local club for me in Haslemere, so it would have been a move that interested me because it would have made life easier in terms of getting to training. Mostly I drove up to Tottenham, but sometimes I got the train, and one morning I did that, I picked up the paper and read in the sports pages that Portsmouth "are very keen on Ron Reynolds". This is how I found out. The club hadn't said a word to me. So immediately after training was over, I went and had a word with Arthur and he said, "Yes, that's right." This was the type of manager he was, he didn't try to sweep it away as newspaper talk as many managers would have done and pretend there was nothing to it. He said, "I must be blunt with you, I've had to turn them down. If they'd had an experienced goalkeeper who they could have let me have in exchange, who could have slotted in in the event of Ted being injured, then I might have been able to let you go. But they haven't got anybody, so I've had to turn them down."

'So I said "Fair enough, that OK, that's all I wanted to know." I understood his position perfectly because obviously his first concern had to be about the well-being of the team as a whole, but he did have the decency to let me know where I stood, and that he sympathised with my position. He didn't make me any empty guarantees that I might be in the first team before long: he made it clear that Ted was still first choice, but that I was good enough to slot straight into the team in his place if he were to get injured. And ultimately that honesty worked in Arthur's favour as it so often did. I think he recognised that I had been in the reserves for too long, and though he didn't actively look to get me a transfer, I think he kept his ears open for a club that I could go to. About two weeks later I was training and he called me in. I went in and he said "You're keen to get away," and I said, "No, I'm not," which I think took him aback. "Well," he said, "bearing in mind our discussion about Portsmouth, Fulham have come after you. They are willing to let me have Ian Black in exchange." Ian was a Scottish goalkeeper, he'd been at Fulham a few years and he had a lot of experience. Arthur told me, "Ian isn't as good a goalkeeper as you are, but he would be a capable reserve and he could play for us and do a good job in the event of anything happening to Ted. Because of that, I would be willing to let you go, under the circumstances. Do you want to go?" So I said, "No thanks," and I think Arthur was pleased about that. But it all came about because he'd been honest with me in the first place and because I felt I could trust him.

'I also felt that I'd done a couple of years in the background at a very good club and that it would take a special kind of move to get me away. Ted was thirty-two or thirty-three by then and he'd had an incredible run without injury. I felt that, sooner or later, my chance would come. Arthur had made it clear that if anything happened to Ted, he wouldn't be looking beyond me to take his place. I'd done my apprenticeship again and I felt I was due some reward for it, if you like.'

So ultimately Pompey plucked Ted Platt from the Arsenal reserves instead and Ron returned to the Tottenham second side. It must have been torturous for him, because, after a false dawn when they won four of their first five games, mediocrity quickly set in amid a first team that was quickly disintegrating, as its players grew old and its manager grew ill. Throughout the 1953/54 season Rowe was not in the best of health, and at times team affairs fell into the hands of assistant manager Jimmy Anderson, the man who had signed Reynolds at Waterloo Station. With the club in a state of some disarray, there were many who looked to the players to provide an element of stability, so changes were few and far between, despite the fact that Tottenham were gradually slipping down the league. The FA Cup promised some relief with early-round wins over Leeds United, Manchester City and, after a struggle, Hull City, but that was snuffed out in the quarter-finals when Tottenham were handed a 3–0 defeat by the tournament's eventual winners, West Bromwich Albion.

With Rowe back at the helm and the season all but dead, Ron finally got his opportunity as Ted Ditchburn went down injured in the spring of 1954, concluding an incredible run of 247 successive games in the Tottenham goal, a record that stretched back over five seasons. Looking back, Ron recalled the excitement he felt at finally getting his chance. 'It came in the latter stages of the season and, like any goalkeeper, any player, I had mixed feelings. I was sad to get the chance because of an injury, especially as it was an injury to a friend, but of course it had been the opportunity that I'd been waiting for ever since I got to Tottenham and I was delighted finally to get into the team after such a long wait.'

The report of Ron's debut, against Sunderland

Ron lined up in the Tottenham goal for the first time in the home game against Sunderland on 20 March. It was a more auspicious occasion than his debut for Aldershot, when he'd conceded seven goals, but not by much. This time he picked the ball out of the back of the net three times as a jaded, end-of-season Spurs side lost to a Sunderland side who had managed just one other away win to that stage – at Arsenal. Sunderland's need for points was more pressing than Tottenham's, since their relegation fears were far more pronounced. Only an impressive final run-in hauled them clear of the drop, leaving them eighteenth, two places beneath Spurs.

There were two further opportunities for Ron, his first away game coming just across London at Stamford Bridge against a Chelsea side whose season was also petering out. (However, they were just twelve months away from securing their solitary league title.) Tottenham put on a solid display but Ron was given a severe testing, which he was more than up to, admitting, 'the game went very well', although Spurs finally went down 1–0. But it was the

Ron saves a Chelsea penalty in the dying minutes, but it's not enough to rescue the game
(A Ronald Traube)

intervention of Alf Ramsey that gave Ron the chance to grab the limelight. 'Four minutes from time Alf gave away a penalty. I thought: He ruddy would do this – four minutes from time! They were lining up on the edge of the penalty box and I can still see Eddie Baily now, pointing to me to tell me to go to my left-hand side. The Chelsea player picked up the ball, walked up and put it down on the spot and Eddie was going mad, trying to tell me which way to dive without anyone seeing him. I thought somebody must have seen him so I blotted him out and went to my right and of course I saved it!'

Tottenham ended the season a mere seven points above the drop zone, proof positive that this was an ailing team that needed to be rebuilt, almost from the bottom up. It was a warning that a club in behind-the-scenes turmoil would fail to heed until it was almost too late.

CHAPTER ELEVEN

1954–55, the Spurs first-team goalkeeper
(Topical Press)

Anybody who imagines that football clubs are beacons of harmony and happiness is, of course, living in a world where the trains run on time, malt whisky is available for free on the National Health and babies take a vow of silence at birth which lasts until they're eighteen. Back on Planet Earth, however, clubs are actually a hotbed of Machiavellian political intrigue, packed with manipulators so cunning that they could give lessons to weasels.

And that shouldn't really be any great surprise – after all, in many ways, a football club is the same as a political party, where everybody wants the unit to be a huge success, but they all want the credit as individuals for achieving it. Unfortunately, clubs have just one manager, in the same way as there can be only one prime minister. But there are plenty of wannabes, all looking to undermine the man at the helm and grab the attention and the place in history. As with politics, so with football. And just as there were those ready to eject

Thatcher and Major, so at Spurs in Ron's time Arthur Rowe was vulnerable. The 1954/55 season would provide the opportunity to administer the final heave to push him over the edge and into unemployment, for things were far from rosy at White Hart Lane.

Football teams, like life itself, can go from the sublime to the ridiculous pretty quickly. Manchester United managed to go from European Cup winners in 1968 to relegation from the First Division within six years. While not quite such a staggering fall, at the start of December 1954, Tottenham Hotspur, who had collected the League Championship trophy in May 1951, were on the brink of returning to the Second Division from whence they'd come just five years earlier. Having put their collective heads in the sand after the trials and tribulations of the previous season, Spurs had, to some extent, fallen back on the old guard for the 1954/55 season, including the recall of the fit-again Ted Ditchburn in goal. But experience could not overcome the problems of physical reduction that the ageing process brings with it, and Tottenham were in seemingly terminal decline at the halfway point of the season. After 21 games, they had 16 points, having gone down to defeat in 11 of their fixtures. But just as damaging as the lack of points was the off-field struggle that was eventually to see the end of Rowe as the Tottenham manager.

Rowe himself was in no position to defend his interests after suffering further bouts of debilitating ill health, problems which Ron Reynolds ascribed to the pressure of work and the faltering nature of his side: 'Arthur was a very nice man as well as a very good tactician and coach, and it hurt him to have to drop players from the team. I suppose there is no room for sentiment when football is all about results, but Arthur took those decisions hard and they worried him a lot. A person like Alf Ramsey who was utterly ruthless when it came to winning games had no qualms about making those sorts of decisions, because he was solely interested in his own success – look at the way he made the decision to drop Greaves for the World Cup Final in 1966 – but for Arthur, I think it hurt him to tell good players that their time was up, that they were no longer wanted, and it played on his nerves.

'His health had deteriorated, people were putting daggers in his

*November 1954, a difficult month
as Spurs slide down the table. Ron
in action against Leicester City (above
and left, Empics); (right) 'Tottenham
Hotspur's goalkeeper Reynolds watches
a penalty shot from Lynn (Aston Villa
right-back) rising, to eventually go up
and over the bar' reads the original
caption (Sport & General)*

back which was really terrible to see. Results got worse and worse because he delayed bringing in new blood and then he had to cope with the pressures of a club that was sinking towards the bottom of the division. And there were plenty of people around the club who were only too happy to see him start to fail. I think it was just a build-up of things that got to him. He had had to stop working for a while in previous seasons because of his health, but though he got through 1954/55, it was obviously a trial for him.'

Football is an incredibly competitive, testosterone-fuelled environment, where men are all trying to outdo one another all the time, trying to push their careers another rung up the ladder. That's one of its attractions: there's always a bigger challenge awaiting you, no matter what you've just achieved. But it's also responsible for the darker side of the game, and the truism that while you make plenty of acquaintances inside football, few make many close friends. How can you when, even while you're working together, you're trying to eclipse your colleagues?

Another truism is that very often the most successful teams have the most volatile dressing rooms, because great talents tend to come with great egos. With immense ability comes a desire to express it, not just on the field of play, but in the dressing room. But assembling good players with commensurate egos is one thing; handling them is something else altogether. In encouraging opinions and expression, it's easy to unleash a genie you can't then push back into the bottle whenever you feel like it. Which is why winning is so important. When things are going well any cracks are papered over, not least because everyone is finding win bonuses in their pay packets. All is fine and disputes can be ignored, or even used as fuel for the fire, as Ron recalls at Tottenham: 'Very often there was out-and-out war between the defenders, and I remember being amazed at this when I first went there from Aldershot. I can recall some absolutely enormous, blazing rows between Alf Ramsey and Bill Nicholson, which was odd really because both didn't have much to say most of the time – unless it was to have an argument. Alf was terrible like that – he didn't suffer what he saw to be fools gladly and he would quickly chew you out if he disagreed with you – but Bill could give as good as he got. Typically dour Yorkshireman, very blunt.

'He got fed up that Alf would cut him out of the game, he'd bypass him and go straight on to the forwards, he'd race upfield and just expect Bill to slot in behind him. Bill only got the one England cap where Alf got dozens and I think Bill sometimes thought that he was winning them for Alf and not getting noticed himself. So they would have these absolutely furious arguments, and I think Arthur was quite pleased to see it, at least initially, because it showed how much they cared about the game.

'Arthur would just say, "Argue it out among yourselves the two of you, I'm not getting involved!" And he would leave them at each other's throat. It wasn't a problem when I first went there, because we won the league and we were up at the top and everything took care of itself. But when you start losing games, the arguments take on a different character, because it isn't about ideas and the game in general, it becomes all about blame: "If you hadn't done that, we wouldn't have lost." Of course, you get that when you're successful too, and then it can be a positive, constructive thing. But when you're down and those arguments go on week after week, it becomes very destructive.

'And with Alf and Bill there was a very strong rivalry because I think both had come to the conclusion that they were going to stay in the game after they'd finished playing and I think they both had designs on staying at Tottenham. But there was never any way the two of them could have stayed on as coaches there. First, you didn't have a whole staff of coaches in a club in those days, but also, it was clear they could never work together as coaches, especially with one senior to the other. And with both coming closer to retiring, that meant there was a real rivalry between them.'

Other rivalries existed at Spurs too, notably between Rowe on the one hand and his assistant Jimmy Anderson, backed by some board members, on the other. Anderson had, of course, had a taste of working as the number one at the club when Rowe had been on the sick list, and many suggested that he wasn't averse to taking on the role full time. Equally, Anderson was looked upon as a more palatable manager by some directors. Even more than today, back in the 1950s football directors tended to undertake a role at a club for the social cachet attached to it as much as for any other reason. After all, it was much better to be able to tell your peers at the local golf club that you were a director at Tottenham than simply to say you were a butcher, baker or candlestick maker. But with Arthur Rowe and his revolutionary push-and-run style of football monopolising the headlines, the directors weren't getting a look-in. With the quieter Anderson at the helm they could step out of the shadows too, not least because, in him, they saw a more malleable character who would do their bidding far more than Rowe ever would. Rowe had bucked the norm which existed in most clubs at the time where the directors informed the manager on Friday morning of what his team would be on the Saturday. While Anderson would never agree to a return to those days, the Spurs board clearly felt he might take the odd bit of advice in that department.

Certainly Ron felt that there were plenty of political shenanigans going on in the background, which didn't help the team's cause: 'There's no doubt that as Arthur's health deteriorated, people around the club were putting daggers in his back, which was really terrible to see, given the man he was and everything that he had done for Tottenham over his time there.'

In fairness to the club and those involved, it was true to say that the side was in decline and in real danger of dropping out of the top flight and it was obvious that changes would have to be made if Tottenham weren't to suffer the ignominy of relegation. The silver lining for Ron was that it meant he was back in the firing line again, replacing Ted Ditchburn in goal. Perhaps the key change, however, came with the arrival of Danny Blanchflower, the successor to Bill Nicholson at right-half and a man who would ultimately call time on Ramsey's career. Blanchflower was a visionary player who believed in football as the glory game – he wasn't simply going to slot in defensively as Ramsey careered up the wing, so Alf's days were numbered.

The signing of Blanchflower was Rowe's last throw of the dice, his last attempt at bringing in his sort of footballer. According to Ron, 'Danny was the icing on the cake. He was exactly the kind of

The 1954 White Hart Lane Christmas Party

player that Arthur loved to see in his teams, one with imagination and intelligence, and I think that by buying him, Arthur was trying to draw a line under that first great team he'd had and was saying that he was ready to start again and build another team in that style.

'I know Arthur said that when Danny came, and we went up to Manchester City to play them and got a 0–0 draw, that it was the first time he'd been able to sit down in the stands and not worry about the game. And we did start to improve quite rapidly from there. By the end of December we were on our way out of trouble. We drew at home to Aston Villa the following Saturday, won at Bolton on Christmas Day, then beat them at home on the Bank Holiday Monday, drew at Sunderland on New Year's Day, and that little run just started to pull us away from things. We felt we were on the right track again. And as things turned out, we took twenty-four points in

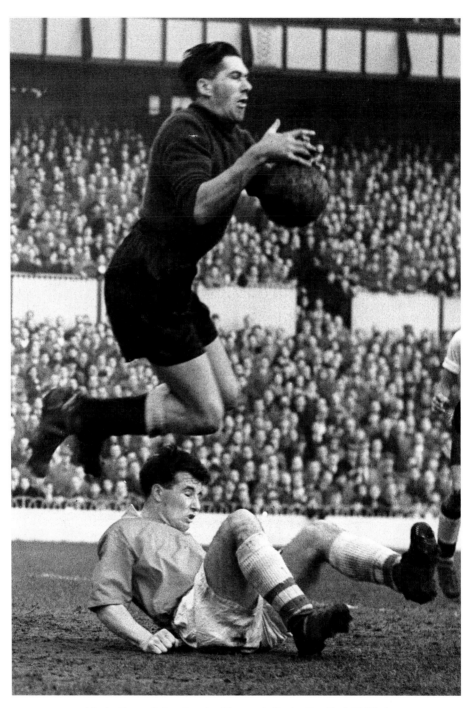

The double over Bolton (completed here on the Boxing Day Bank Holiday) saw Spurs turn the corner (Sport & General)

the second half of the season, which, since Chelsea won the championship with just fifty-two points, was almost championship form. The only disappointment was in the FA Cup, when we lost 3–1 at York in the fifth round, because we really felt that the way we were playing after Christmas, we could have gone on and won the cup.'

From a romantic point of view, it would be nice to believe that the arrival of Blanchflower and the renaissance that followed was all down to Spurs playing the sort of sweet, flowing football that had been their trademark in the glory years at the start of the 1950s. But, as Ron recalled, when relegation stares you in the face, it's pragmatism that managers call upon as their first line of defence: 'I know that Danny believed he was coming to a club that was all about push and run, high footballing principles and so on. He was a terrific fan of Arthur Rowe and had always admired Tottenham from the first time he saw them when he came over from Northern Ireland. I remember him saying to me that he could never understand why the English went so overboard about the Hungarians and their revolutionary style of play in 1953, when Spurs had been playing that way for years.

'But when Danny got to Tottenham, it was a different club. Arthur was in decline, on the way out really, and we were just looking to get as many points as we could in whatever way was necessary. When you're in trouble, you change. To a certain extent, push and run as a method of playing was no longer successful because we didn't have the players who had made it work. We no longer had effervescent Eddie Baily, who buzzed

—P.A. Reuters.

Down in the snow dives Tottenham Hotspur goalkeeper Reynolds to take the ball off the toe of Arsenal inside-right Tapscott during the First Division game at White Hart Lane, London, on January 15th, when 26 Football League games were postponed or abandoned.

around, loved the push-and-run idea, just his style, of course. So it was with Alf Ramsey and Ronnie Burgess: push and run suited them, but they were either going or gone and the players who came in took time to adapt and replace them.

'When you play a one-touch, quick-moving, passing kind of game, you rely on confidence, and that comes from experience and from results. We had new players in there and the results were poor, so the confidence wasn't there and we had to resort to a more English style of play, getting the ball from the defence to the front players as quickly as possible, bypassing the half-backs, which hadn't been our game before. But at that stage, it was just a case of getting out of trouble. Once we'd done that, towards the end of the season, Arthur tried to bring us back towards that push-and-run idea again, but it was too late.'

CHAPTER TWELVE

The start of a great Cup run, Spurs 4–0 Boston Utd,
7th January 1956 (Sport & General)

By season's end on 5 May 1955, when Spurs won 1–2 at Charlton Athletic, they'd hauled themselves up to sixteenth and accumulated forty points. Not inspiring statistics, but in a poor First Division season they were more remarkable than they might seem at first glance. Given their dismal first half of the campaign, they'd improved drastically: they may have been only five points clear of relegation, but equally they were the same number of points away from the respectability of eighth. To the casual observer, then, Spurs seemed to have weathered the storm and had begun to rebuild successfully.

For Arthur Rowe, though, that sea change in fortune had come much too late. Driven to the edge of a breakdown by the pressures on and off the field at White Hart Lane, having led Tottenham to safety he left the club he had done so much to build. He left it in the care of his assistant, Jimmy Anderson, who was immediately elevated to the top job, to the disquiet of some members of the playing staff, including Ron: 'I'd had a good run in the team under Arthur. I played twenty-six games in the First Division at a time when the team had turned the corner, I was in the side right through to the end of the season and I felt as if I'd become the first choice ahead of Ted Ditchburn, which had been something I'd been working towards ever since I'd joined the club. I was sure that under Arthur I would be our first-choice goalkeeper. Under Jimmy Anderson it was a question of starting all over again – that's why players always seemed to be so insecure, because their own futures were so much out of their own hands, whatever their level of performance.'

That was never more obvious than in the first weeks of the Anderson reign. 'When Anderson took over, Bill Nicholson took his chance and hung up his boots to take on the role of assistant manager,' recalled Ron, 'freeing the space in the team for Danny Blanchflower. I think Bill always had in mind that if he wanted to stay at Tottenham as a coach, he had to get in before Alf Ramsey did. With Bill being that bit older, it meant he could retire earlier and he took advantage of the fact that Arthur had gone to move up to assist Anderson. And, let's face it, Anderson needed all the help he could get because he was hopeless!

'I already felt a bit unhappy about things with Arthur having left because, although he was the manager, I felt he was also an ally for me. We had similar views on the game and I'd finally come into the side and done well for him. I was also very close friends very quickly with Danny Blanchflower, who was obviously an Arthur man. I thought we were going to be able to take things forward, so to have Anderson take charge was worrying right from the start, and he underlined that pretty quickly because he was a much more ruthless sort of character.

'Alf Ramsey had played for Tottenham for years, he had done great things and the club had done great things, but eventually things started to go wrong. In that first close season under Anderson, as soon as he and Bill were appointed, we went off on tour to Hungary. The list of personnel who were going out there was put up on the noticeboard and, much to everyone's surprise, one person was not included in the tour, and that was Alf! At the time it was assumed that this was due to Anderson and Nicholson, with them wanting to exert their authority. Alf was the senior pro there, and perhaps the two of them saw him as their biggest threat. If things didn't go right over the next couple of seasons again, perhaps Alf might be waiting there to take over from them.

'When Alf wasn't included on the tour to Hungary, it was a bitter blow. We never got to the bottom of it but I know all the players at the time agreed that this was a rough trick to play on him, being turfed out like that. Later on, and I don't know if this were true or not, it was said that he knew he was going to Ipswich and it was this that stopped him from going on the tour. But I am not sure about that. While we went off to Hungary, he went to coach in Rhodesia that summer and then he did leave the club to go to Ipswich as manager. But I don't think that had ever been his intention. I'm sure he had intended to continue playing for Spurs for at least another season. I think it was simply the case that Anderson didn't want any threat to his position at the club because he knew that he wasn't really good enough to take over from Arthur.'

Ditchburn returned to the side under Anderson, but it was to be a brief renaissance as Spurs' old failings consigned them to another season of struggle. They managed just one point from the first twelve in a desperate opening run that left them rooted to the bottom of the First Division and staring relegation in the face from the outset. Ultimately Ron was recalled to the colours and enjoyed what turned out to be perhaps his greatest year at White Hart Lane. He racked up twenty-eight appearances in the Division One season as well as being an ever present in another great FA Cup run that took Tottenham to the semi-finals. But, as Ron recalled, given that he never saw eye to eye with Anderson, and was scarcely more friendly with Bill Nicholson, his recall emphasised the dire straits in which Spurs found themselves. 'Bill was a very dour man and hard to get to know. But, in fairness to him, it has to be very hard for you to go from being one of the boys in the dressing room to suddenly being the manager, the man who sets the tactics, sets discipline, calls all the shots. It's not easy being in charge of men whom you were team-

A pre-season photoshoot with Danny Blanchflower and Ted Ditchburn, August 1955 (Empics)

mates with, and that made for uneasy relationships, especially when I tried to make a stand on their behalf. It used to be said that if Anderson signed a player, whoever it might be, then that player could do no wrong. Well, if that were the case, then I was the first exception! Anderson had signed me all those years ago in that railway station restaurant, but that was the high point of our relationship.' Ron attributed that antipathy to the fact that he spent some of his time at Tottenham working as the players' representative on the Players' Union, or the Professional Footballers' Association as it is now known. In those repressive days, when the clubs held all the cards when it came to players' contracts, they were very unwilling to give away any of their advantage and, at best, saw the union reps as irritating trouble-makers. At worst, they viewed the reps as little more than communist agitators, working away as moles inside the game, and attempting to bring it crashing to the floor.

'I had problems with Anderson, and then with Nicholson,

because I represented the union,' recalled Ron. 'As soon as Anderson took over, I got into conflict with him on a matter regarding Tony Marchi. He'd signed as a professional for the club in June 1950, a month before me. In those days, players were not as well paid as they are now: it was the time of the maximum wage and we got something just above the average wage for a skilled worker in a factory. They did not have the testimonial system at the time, but they did use benefits as a reward for loyalty. If you'd been at a club for five years, you were entitled to up to a hundred and fifty pounds per year (up to a maximum of seven hundred and fifty pounds) for each of those years, which was a very nice top-up. It was like getting nine months' extra pay at the end of that five years, which was important for people whose careers would be finished at the age of thirty-five and who would then have to start again. After you'd had your first benefit, if you were at the club another five years, you could get another benefit of up to a thousand pounds, which was a lot of money in those days: a year's salary, pretty much. Players looked on that benefit money as being something they could put into a pension, or perhaps use to set them up in business. Lots of players would go off and buy a sports shop or start running a pub with that money once they'd finished playing.

'Tony had played more games in those five years than I had. He'd had two full seasons in the team after he took over from Ronnie Burgess, but when it came to giving him his benefit money, all they'd pay him was five hundred pounds. This was a man who'd taken over from the club captain and who they'd make the captain later. That was one thing, but then a few weeks later, when I'd completed *my* five years' service with the club, but had played perhaps half as many games as Tony had, they gave me the full seven hundred and fifty pounds, which was incredible.

'I assumed at the time, and still do, that they gave me the full payoff to keep me quiet as the players' rep. They thought if they looked after me, then I'd do the same for them: a "You scratch my back" kind of arrangement.'

If Anderson genuinely did think that would be the case, it suggests that he was a poor reader of character. As Ron had shown in the past, and would continue to show for the rest of his life, if he came across injustice, he simply would not accept it and would always fight it. It was a trait which made him the ideal representative for the players, but a nightmare for the club.

'As the representative of the Players' Union, I had a job to do. Apart from that, simply out of common decency, I felt it was only right that I fought on Tony's behalf. So I went to town on this because it was crazy, absolutely crazy. Anderson had me in his office and said, "Look after your own interests – he won't thank you for it. You look after yourself or else you'll be in trouble. Worry about the others and you'll be for it," but that was just unacceptable. I said to him, "What do you think I'm in this position for if it isn't to look after other people's interests?"

'We never got on after that, because, a bit like Danny Blanch-flower, I was something of a rebel. The only difference between Danny's idea of being a rebel and mine was that he was much more diplomatic. He used to say, "Simmer down! Take it easy, you'll get there!" But we both had a basic belief that you fought for every-body's rights. It used to be terrific to watch how he worked. He'd have been a great politician as far as that side of things was con-cerned.

'But even Danny couldn't get past Anderson, I'm afraid. Anderson was an individual who kow-towed very much to the directors – he'd always been that type. And that was the beginning of the end for me as far as Anderson was concerned, although he had to stick by me as he had nobody else at the time to put in goal because Ted was well into his thirties and starting to suffer injuries, too.'

The suspicion with which the Players' Union was viewed was inevitable, given the backgrounds of most directors and the social climate that still persisted in the early 1950s. Post-war Britain was witnessing a titanic struggle between the forces of change and the forces of the establishment as a desire for modernity collided with a reactionary desire to maintain the status quo. As far as football clubs were concerned, the bulk of their directors were drawn from the old school, from moneyed families who saw themselves as benefactors towards the common man and his common game. They were joined by a smattering of nouveau riche businessmen, locals who had made good, dragged themselves up by the proverbial bootstraps and made a few quid. Having made their way into the upper echelons of society thanks to hard work, they certainly weren't going to let the tide of history sweep away their hard-won, new-found privileges without a fight.

Whichever group they belonged to, old money or new, the majority certainly weren't at home with the great unwashed and the increasing demands of a workforce tired of making huge profits for their employers without ever being given the chance to put their own noses into the trough and enjoy the fruits of their labours. To many employers, the answer to the question 'What about the workers?' was simple: 'What about them?' Consequently, the employer–employee relationship, or the us-and-them outlook that disfigured British industry for years, was not a happy or healthy one, with the trade unions and their adherents simply beyond the pale.

This philosophy was destined to end in tears, particularly as players laboured under the most stringent restrictions: not allowed to earn more than the maximum wage that ultimately struggled up to £24 a week by the late 1950s, however good they were or whatever prizes they won; and unable to leave their club for a new challenge, better conditions or greater opportunity to win medals, unless their club chose to sell them. No wonder it was termed 'soccer slavery'. The authorities and the players were on a collision course, especially as nothing was sacred any more. The war had swept away many of the vestiges of the Victorian and Edwardian ages, and the onset of the American age and the rock 'n' roll generation was getting rid of the rest. The football establishment's nemesis took an odd shape: a pointed-chinned player who toiled in the Fulham engine room alongside the more spectacular talent of Johnny Haynes, the man destined to become the first £100-a-week footballer. His less gifted, but infinitely more strident, colleague, Jimmy Hill, was the man who would eventually drag football kicking and screaming into the modern age, heading the union as it secured the long-overdue abolition of the maximum wage and the end to the restrictive contracts which cemented a player to his club.

Hill was an agitator extraordinaire and one whom Reynolds admired, in that role at least, simply because he believed that it was time players got a fair deal instead of a raw one. It wasn't for nothing that Ron kept hold of an article by Hill that appeared in the *FA News*, under the title, 'Apropos The Pro'.

'The average wage of professional footballers is £1 or so more than the average wage in industry. So although he may be on a public pedestal, the footballer's purchasing power is no larger than his neighbour's, and his neighbour knows it.

'Unlike the man next door, he must perform in public before perhaps a million people in a season, as well as having to contend with eleven opponents who do their utmost to ensure he makes a mess of his job.

'Sometimes, publicly, he is a hero. In the nature of things he must at times look a blundering fool. If he should fail continually, a Club will never hesitate to barter his wages down or transfer him to a lower grade, sapping his confidence in himself as a player and a man.

'If he reaches the stars, the Football League allow him to be paid £1,250 per annum and the Football Association a little extra for international appearances. What a pitiful attempt this is to instil into our ambitious young men the confidence to go out as giants and beat the world. What a shameful advertisement it is to attract young men of higher intellectual ability into a great sport.'

Powerful stuff, but accurate, for the stereotype of the thick footballer, which endures still, had its roots in those days. If you were a lad with intelligence, football was hardly the most lucrative avenue for a bright young thing, and it was rare to find players as canny as Reynolds and Blanchflower. If you had brain cells, better use them in the professions rather than as a professional footballer.

By the start of November Ron was back in goal for the visit of Cardiff City, with a new, young team in front of him, as he remembered: 'Maurice Norman was a very good player, and his arrival [at full-back] was just more recognition that the old days were over and that we had to create a new team for the future or lose our way. Ramsey and Baily went, Clarke went, Bobby Smith and Maurice came in, Danny was settling into the side, I started to play regularly

ALDERSHOT TOWN. v. BRISTOL CITY.

This was the first win for Aldershot at home since November 24th 1944.

Bristol scored for after 10 minutes.

After half time Brooks scored two for Aldershot.

The match was a strong fight right to the end.

Crowse numbered 4,000.

LDERSHOT TOWN.

Bristol City Football Club Ltd.
— Ashton Gate —
1945 - 46

Chairman:
ENKINS.

Secretary:
R. HEWISON

this match & were
match apart from 2i

day,
HT

was cheered
he match.
once, when
gone on to.
ld have
a penalty

R
Mr.

Robi

A typical entry from Ron's scrapbook
and (photograph) making a save at the Recreation Ground.

TOL C
n eigh
o the
clev
stro
t missed the goalshots
in good shots
st missed the goalpost.
d Beauchamp were Alder-
t dangerous wingers
eld the upper hand and
in the last ten minutes
Chilcott and Curran.
were indebted to Rey-
did brilliantly in goal.

more forcefully. Bristol
more forceful side. Clark
ams getting in good shots

RIGHT

IE MATCH
RQUAY UNITED

The
VILLA
news and record
3d

THE FOOTBALL LEAGUE — FIRST DIVISION
SATURDAY, NOVEMBER 26th, 1955
TOTTENHAM HOTSPUR
Match No. 19 — Kick-off 2-15 p.m.

МОСКОВСКИЙ ГОРОДСКОЙ СОВЕТ
СОЮЗА СПОРТИВНЫХ ОБЩЕСТВ И ОРГАНИЗАЦИЙ РСФСР
ЦЕНТРАЛЬНЫЙ СТАДИОН имени В. И. ЛЕНИНА

ФУТБОЛ

МЕЖДУНАРОДНАЯ ВСТРЕЧА

27
МАЯ
1959 г.

„ТОТТЕНХЭМ ХОТСПУРС"
(ЛОНДОН)
— „ТОРПЕДО"
(МОСКВА)

BRISTOL ROVERS
FOOTBALL CLUB LTD.

FOOTBALL LEAGUE SECOND DIVISION

OFFICIAL PROGRAMME 3d

BRISTOL STADIUM · EASTVILLE

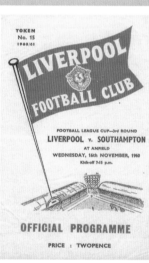

TOKEN
No. 15
1960/61

LIVERPOOL
FOOTBALL CLUB

FOOTBALL LEAGUE CUP—3rd ROUND
LIVERPOOL v. SOUTHAMPTON
AT ANFIELD
WEDNESDAY, 16th NOVEMBER, 1960
Kick-off 7-15 p.m.

OFFICIAL PROGRAMME

PRICE : TWOPENCE

Official souvenir programme
CORONATION CUP
First Roun

19 53

CELTIC v.
ARSENAL
AT HAMPDEN PARK
Monday, 11th May, 1953

HIBERNIAN v.
TOTTENHAM HOTSPU
AT IBROX STADIUM
Kick-off 7 pm

COPYRIGHT ALL RIGHTS RESERVED
TOTTENHAM HOTSPUR
FOOTBALL AND ATHLETIC COMPANY LIMITED

Official Programme
AND RECORD OF THE CLUB

PRICE
TWOPENCE

VOL. XLVIII. No. 32 SATURDAY, JANUARY 7th, 1956

BOSTON'S CUP-TIE VISIT

OUR BAND WILL PLAY AT EACH HOME GAME

HIBERNIAN F.C. PROGRAMME

VOL. 6. No. 39. MONDAY, 14th MARCH, 1955 Kick-off 7-15 p.m.

Floodlight Challenge Match

HIBERNIAN VERSUS
TOTTENHAM HOTSPUR 6d

ALDERSHOT & DISTRICT
TRACTION Co.

COACHES for HIRE
EXPRESS COACH SERVICE
LONDON

Aldershot Football Club Ltd.
Official Programme
PRICE TWOPENCE
Number 28 Saturday, December 31st, 1949

T. WICKENDEN
& SON LTD.
Builders' Merchants
St. GEORGE'S RD. EAST
ALDERSHOT

WALLPAPERS, BORDERS,
CORNERS, DISTEMPER,
PAINTS, TILE SURROUNDS,
CEMENT, SAND & BALLAST
always in stock.

The
Central Commercial
Hotel & Restaurant

STATION ROAD

Programmes from Ron's extensive collection of all the matches he played in.

Nottingham Forest FOOTBALL CLUB
City Ground, Nottingham

Football Association Challenge Cup – 6th Round
Saturday, 30th March, 1963

Nottingham Forest
v.
Southampton

OFFICIAL **6d.** PROGRAMME

No. 45
MONDAY, 29th APRIL, 1957

BURNLEY FOOTBALL CLUB
SEASON 1956 - 1957

F.A. CUP WINNERS 1913 - 1914
F.A. CUP FINALISTS 1946 - 1947

CHAMPIONS: Div. I, 1920-21; Div. II, 1897-98
RUNNERS-UP: Div. I, 1919-20; Div. II, 1912-13, 1946-47
WINNERS, LANCASHIRE CUP: 1890, 1914-15, 1949-50, 1951-52

OFFICIAL **3d** PROGRAMME
PUBLISHED BY BURNLEY FOOTBALL & ATHLETIC CO. LTD.

UNITED REVIEW
MANCHESTER UNITED FOOTBALL CLUB

MANCHESTER UNITED
v
TOTTENHAM HOTSPUR
kick-off 3 pm

6th APRIL
4d.
NUMBER 30

1956-57 SEASON

OFFICIAL PROGRAMME

Sunday Express Pictures

LEEDS UNITED A.F.C.

versus

SOUTHAMPTON
SATURDAY, 29th SEPTEMBER, 1962

OFFICIAL PROGRAMME **4d**

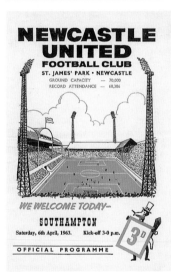

NEWCASTLE UNITED FOOTBALL CLUB
ST. JAMES' PARK • NEWCASTLE
GROUND CAPACITY — 70,000
RECORD ATTENDANCE — 68,386

WE WELCOME TODAY—
SOUTHAMPTON
Saturday, 6th April, 1963.   Kick-off 3-0 p.m.

OFFICIAL PROGRAMME **3d**

Offizielles Programm 50 Rp.

Fussballstadion St. Jakob
Mittwoch, 23. Oktober
Trainingsspiel der Nationalmannschaft
18.30 Uhr:

Concordia
Nationalmannschaft B

20.15 Uhr:

Schweiz A - Tottenham Hotspurs London

OFFICIAL
Albion NEWS
& PROGRAMME

3d

West Bromwich Albion Football Club, Limited

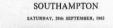

President: The Right Hon. The Earl of Dartmouth, G.C.V.O., E.D., D.L.

Vol. 48 No. 35 (Copyright)   March 9th, 1957

SOUTHAMPTON FOOTBALL CLUB
FOUNDED 1885

Match No. 10

Saturday, October 29 1960

NORWICH C.

Official PROGRAMME **4d**

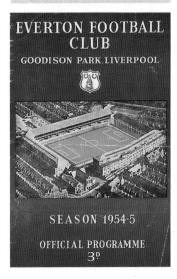

EVERTON FOOTBALL CLUB
GOODISON PARK, LIVERPOOL

SEASON 1954-5

OFFICIAL PROGRAMME
3d

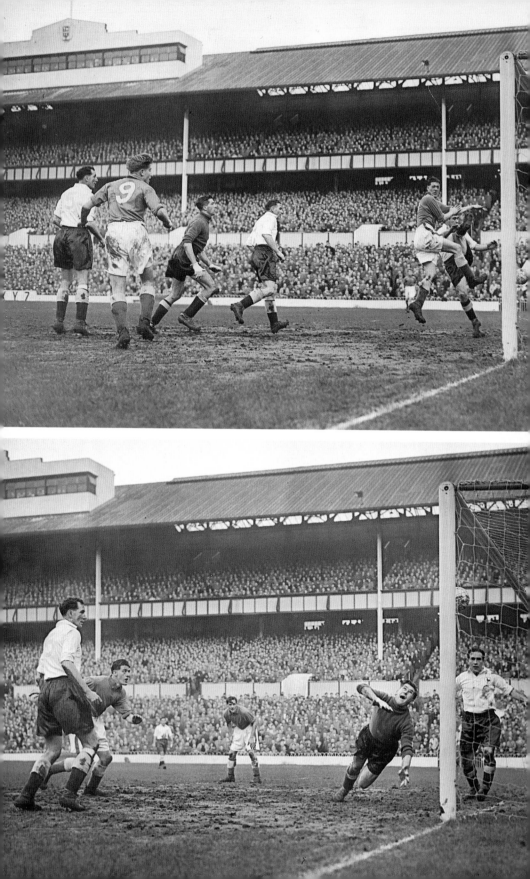

Everton put three past Spurs and Ron, at White Hart lane, 4 December 1954. Alf Ramsey can only watch (bottom left. Reuters and Sport General).

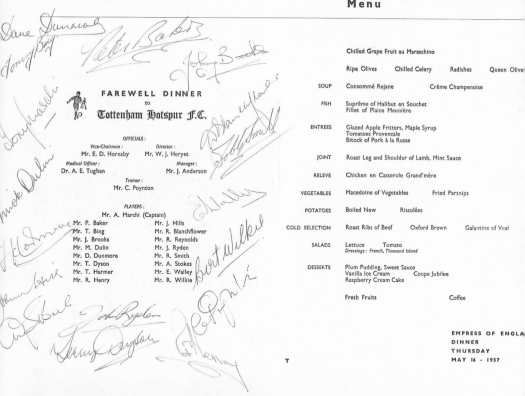

FAREWELL DINNER
to
Tottenham Hotspur F.C.

OFFICIALS:

Vice-Chairman:
Mr. E. D. Hornsby

Director:
Mr. W. J. Heryet

Medical Officer:
Dr. A. E. Tughan

Manager:
Mr. J. Anderson

Trainer:
Mr. C. Poynton

PLAYERS:
Mr. A. Marchi (Captain)

Mr. P. Baker	Mr. J. Hills
Mr. T. Bing	Mr. R. Blanchflower
Mr. J. Brooks	Mr. R. Reynolds
Mr. M. Dulin	Mr. J. Ryden
Mr. D. Dunmore	Mr. R. Smith
Mr. T. Dyson	Mr. A. Stokes
Mr. T. Harmer	Mr. E. Walley
Mr. R. Henry	Mr. R. Wilkie

Chilled Grape Fruit au Maraschino

Ripe Olives   Chilled Celery   Radishes   Queen Olive

SOUP	Consommé Rejane Crème Champenoise
FISH	Suprême of Halibut en Souchet Fillet of Plaice Meunière
ENTREES	Glazed Apple Fritters, Maple Syrup Tomatoes Provencale Bitock of Pork à la Russe
JOINT	Roast Leg and Shoulder of Lamb, Mint Sauce
RELEVE	Chicken en Casserole Grand'mère
VEGETABLES	Macedoine of Vegetables Fried Parsnips
POTATOES	Boiled New Rissolées
COLD SELECTION	Roast Ribs of Beef Oxford Brawn Galantine of Veal
SALADS	Lettuce Tomato Dressings: French, Thousand Island
DESSERTS	Plum Pudding, Sweet Sauce Vanilla Ice Cream Coupe Jubilee Raspberry Cream Cake

Fresh Fruits   Coffee

EMPRESS OF ENGLA
DINNER
THURSDAY
MAY 16 - 1957

THE Lilywhite

OCTOBER 1957

THE OFFICIAL ORGAN OF THE SPURS SUPPORTERS CLUB

Affiliated to the National Federation of Supporters' Clubs

VOL. 8 No. 2   Headquarters: The White Hart Hotel, High Road, Tottenham, N.17   PRICE 6d

MEET THE SPURS AT HOME

introduces this month
RON REYNOLDS

RON, BETTY, DAVID and PETER

Also in this issue:
NEW TEAM PHOTO   ✳   TWO JOHN JONES
IN PLACE OF THE COMBINATION   ✳   CLUB NOTES

The menu (and team signatures) from the *Empress of England* (which took the Spurs first-team squad across the Atlantic in 1957).

While out in Vancouver, August '57, Ron hooked up
with a family originally from Haslemere.

WITH THE COMPLIMENTS OF **Ty·Phoo** LTD., BIRMINGHAM 5
Tea

SOUTHAMPTON F.C.

Back row, L to R: Chivers, Kirby, Reynolds, Godfrey, Traynor, Huxford. *Centre:* White, Williams, Dean, Knapp, Wimshurst, Davies, Gallagher (Trainer),
Front row, L to R: McGuigan, Paine, O'Brien, Chadwick, Mr. Bates (Manager), Hollywood, Burnside, Sydenham, Penk

SOUTHAMPTON

RON REYNOLDS TESTIMONIAL

Southampton F.C.   v   Chelsea F.C.

DINNER

Chilled Honeydew Melon

Cream Portugaise

————————

Fillet of Lemon Sole Bretonne

————————

Roast Saddle of Lamb Orloff
Green Peas
Olivette Potatoes

————————

Soufflé en Surprise

————————

Coffee

————————

Wednesday, April 29th 1964.

again, and you had people like Terry Dyson and Ron Henry starting to play as well. Bringing Maurice in was very important, not only then, but later, when he moved to centre-half, because he was such a good player on the ball, not just a defensive tackler, but a real footballer, which was the way Spurs liked to play, bringing it out from the back. From there, the season was very like the one before: we started to pull away from the bottom of the table, though not as far as we wanted, and we went on a very good run in the FA Cup.'

With his return to the first team seemingly secure, Ron began to enjoy what his position offered to him, and started to take his young son to games at White Hart Lane, as David Reynolds remembers: 'Dad used to take me up to some home games. I could have been only five or six at the time. It was strange, I suppose, because people didn't do that. It was certainly a memorable thing for me. There I was, a kid in a changing room with all these famous players, and even now the smell of the changing room is sort of in my blood.

'In those days, it was quite primitive compared with what you have now. There was liniment everywhere, and that sets off my memory even now when I smell it. The changing rooms weren't that brilliant, very raucous obviously, a lot of swearing and cursing, but not much in the way of tactics or anything like that. I presume they must have done all of that out at the training ground in the week before. I remember there were always cups of tea there before the game and at half-time. I also got to sit in the dug-out during the games. I was the only kid on the touchline during the games, so it was a real honour.

'I think Dad liked that side of it, the things you could do because of your position as a player. He was well aware of the fact that we didn't see a lot of him because of his profession and I think he liked to make up for that when he could. He did a lot of travelling, with forty-two games a season and reserve matches and the FA Cup. Back then they thought nothing of the number of games because it was the norm, even though they weren't getting fortunes for doing it. And, of course, travelling was much harder then. Manchester United might fly down now if they're playing Southampton and stay in the best hotels. In the 1950s if Spurs were at Newcastle, it was

(Facing page, from top) The FA Cup 1956. Key Spurs players Maurice Norman, 1, Len Duquemin, 2, Blanchflower and Ron have a Saturday lunchtime run prior to the fourth-round tie at home to Middlesbrough, 25th January '56 (The Times); West Ham put one past Ron in the sixth round, but Spurs win 2–1 (Sport & General); with the fans prior to the 1956 FA Cup Semi-Final at Villa Park (Spurs lost 1–0 to Man City); (this page) Danny Blanchflower leads Ron and the team out at the Semi-Final at Villa Park (Sport & General); but Spurs go down 1–0 to Manchester City (P. P. Skivington)

a day to travel there, a stopover in a B & B, they'd play at three o'clock on Saturday afternoon and if they were lucky, they'd get back into White Hart Lane at about two in the morning and then have to find their own ways home.'

Once Spurs repeated their trick of the previous season and gradually found their form, the FA Cup began to take on its traditional importance as the team looked to make their first appearance in a Wembley final. The omens early in the competition were good. Boston United were beaten 3–0, Middlesbrough 5–1, Doncaster Rovers 2–0 and then, after a replay, West Ham United went down 1–2 at Upton Park. Spurs were in another semi-final, against Manchester City and their supposedly unstoppable Revie Plan, which featured the future Leeds and England boss playing in the Hungarian style, as a deep-lying centre-forward. It was to be a seminal point for the club and its future, though its value could hardly be appreciated on the day as Tottenham slipped out of the competition, losing 1–0 to a Bobby Johnstone goal at Villa Park. The match remained etched on Ron's memory, though: 'Tommy Harmer had been one of the stars of the show in that run for us, but Anderson didn't like him much, and for some reason, for the semi-final, he changed the team and left out Tommy, and it was no surprise that we didn't look like getting a goal. Danny was the captain at the time and with about fifteen minutes to go, he told Maurice Norman to go up front and play as an attacker in an effort to get the goal back, which is fair enough in a cup tie. But

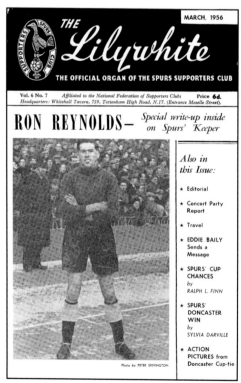

Anderson was sitting in the stands and the directors were asking him what authority Danny had to be doing that – he'd done it in another game previously, I think – and that was it for Anderson. He didn't like to have to answer those questions, so to try to stamp his authority on things, he took the captaincy away from Danny not long after that. He thought that was a show of strength, but really it was weakness, and, eventually, even the directors came to see that. Things went better the following season, but it was the beginning of the end for Anderson. And not before time!'

Spurs saw out the 1955/56 season in eighteenth place, three points shy of the previous year's points total on thirty-seven, and just two points above the drop. Clearly getting rid of Arthur Rowe had not been the answer, but Anderson would almost hit upon a successful formula the following year, masking his own failings as a manager, much to the frustration of the likes of Blanchflower and Reynolds, who could see straight through him. But Ron would have other worries on his mind before long, as his injury jinx reared its ugly head once again.

CHAPTER THIRTEEN

Ron fists the ball away, v Blackpool, 27th April 1957 (Empics)

Going into the 1956/57 season, if Ron Reynolds hadn't entirely succeeded in consigning the name of Ted Ditchburn to the White Hart Lane history books, he had at least put himself ahead of the former England keeper in the Tottenham pecking order, having played more games than his rival in both of the preceding seasons. Unfortunately, as a nostalgic profile of Ron in a Spurs programme of the late 1960s said, with classic understatement, 'You could hardly call Reynolds a lucky player. After the long spell of waiting in the wings as deputy to Ditchburn he sustained a head injury that meant wearing contact lenses when playing.'

Forty-five years ago, contact lenses were not the disposable fashion accessories that they've become today, as Ron's son David explains: 'I remember when I was young he'd had an injury and suddenly needed to start wearing glasses to see properly. That was fine at home, but obviously on the field, you couldn't have a goalkeeper wearing glasses because of the chance of them getting broken. So he got himself fitted out with a pair of contact lenses, but you wouldn't believe them if you saw them. They weren't the filmy little things you've got now. They were these great glass saucer-type things and they were so big you wondered how the hell anybody got it in their eyes. I used to think: Jesus, this is dangerous! But he just used to get on with it, and I suppose after a while it became second nature to him. But the sight of them used to frighten me.

'I assume that because of the way they were made and the sheer size of them, once he had managed to put them in, it would have been hard to dislodge them. Now you see players stopping a game because they've lost one, but I don't think those would have come out very easily. But they must have been really dangerous for a goal-keeper, because he was going headlong down at people's feet, going up for crosses, getting whacked by centre-forwards, but he seemed to get on OK.'

While Ron adapted to his new lenses quite quickly, their size wasn't the only problem that he had to contend with, as new ideas came into the game, notably floodlights, which made midweek football a new and exciting possibility. That was a fresh challenge for Reynolds and his lenses, and one which put him at a genuine disadvantage, as David recalls: 'Those were the early days of floodlighting, and I know he had trouble with that because the lights were quite primitive in many places. I don't think wearing those lenses was really any different to wearing glasses. If you have glasses on under floodlights, there is such a lot of glare if you look up into them, even with the better lights you have now, and if it rains, it's worse, because you end up seeing two or three balls. The lenses weren't much better than that. So coming and catching a ball under lights must have been incredibly difficult. There were no concessions to the dark, they still played with the brown ball at night, the leather soaked up the water, so you could easily lose it.

'He also had trouble if the conditions were humid. Because the lenses were so big, if you got any air trapped underneath, which you could, they'd steam up, and you'd get a fog coming over in front of your eyes. It was an absolute nightmare for him, and I'm sure that at Spurs the management always wondered if they could totally trust him in certain conditions once he started wearing them. Managers like to use the same goalkeeper all the time, so, for the sake of continuity, he might have lost out because they'd always be thinking about having to drop him for night games or if it were especially wet. It certainly didn't do his career any good.'

Fortunately, most goalkeepers didn't suffer the same concussion problems on the same scale as Ron, and so didn't have to go through the contact-lens trauma, but they did often find themselves 'in the wars'. The game was much more physical, while the number 1 was left unprotected by the laws of the game and by the referees who administered them, as David Reynolds remembers: 'Dad did get a lot of knocks to the head in particular, but that was the way goal-keepers were in those days: they'd go diving in at players' feet, which perhaps you see a bit less of today. Saying that, if they go down now, the attacker will generally try to pull away from the ball if he thinks he's going to catch the keeper. When they do clash, you normally see all the defenders ganging up on the attacker, so it's become pretty much unacceptable now for a forward to go for a loose ball and catch the goalie in the process. When Dad was playing, that wasn't the way it was. If a ball was there, the forward had to go for it, that was the expected thing. So if the keeper went down at his feet, chances were he was going to get a crack on the head. And if he did, it would hurt, because players weren't wearing the lightweight boots they have now. They were wearing things that weren't that far from the hobnailed boots that blokes in factories were wearing. If you got kicked by one of them, you stayed kicked.

'The way the goalkeepers were treated was very different as well. It wasn't just the collisions on the ground that caused trouble; the ones off the ground were the most dangerous. If a cross came into the box and the goalkeeper came and collected it, that wasn't an end to it as it is now. Dad might get pole-axed while he was in the air or he might get flattened once he'd got the ball in his hands by a forward trying to charge him into the net. Players certainly weren't as well looked-after then as they are now. If you get a bang on the head now, it's taken very seriously. The ball's put out of play immediately, the trainer comes on and if there's any question of concussion, you're straight off and it's compulsory that you stay out of the game for a week or two to get better. They didn't worry about things like that in those days. All that happened was the trainer would ask you, "How many fingers am I holding up?" If you could count them, that was it, they'd send you straight back out there.'

Ron was back in action for the 1956/57 season, but less frequently than in the two previous terms, in part because Spurs suddenly re-emerged as a more forceful First Division unit after those years in the wilderness. According to Ron, 'There was no particular reason why the team did so much better than in the previous couple of years, because tactically we were nothing impressive. Push and run had gone by the board and we were playing a more direct style that suited some players but not others. I think the main thing was that in the previous year a lot of the necessary changes had been made with the bringing in of Norman, Henry, Dyson and the like. Players like them and Danny Blanchflower were so good that you couldn't help but improve really, no matter what the manager was doing, especially with Bill Nicholson alongside him, because Bill was a very good coach. And there were more changes, with Terry Medwin replacing Sonny Walters, Alfie Stokes in for Johnny Brooks, so the team was freshened up and players with ambition came in.

'I don't think it was a vintage First Division, apart from Manchester United, who absolutely walked the league, and so there was an opportunity for sides to do well if they got it right. I think the big difference was that the team got off to a very good start. The importance of that is often underestimated, but if you do get a few wins under your belt early on, you have that momentum going and you grow in confidence, and confidence is more important than anything.'

Spurs certainly enjoyed their best start in years, picking up seven points from eight in August by beating Leeds and Manchester City at home, drawing at Maine Road and winning at Preston. Disappointing defeats at Blackpool and Bolton took the shine off things, but further wins in September at Villa Park and Roker Park, along with wins at home against Luton and Wolves meant that they could look ahead instead of over their shoulders.

Ted Ditchburn had again become an important part of the team, thanks to Ron's health problems, but Spurs remained fragile, a fact underlined by a defeat at Bournemouth in the fifth round of the FA Cup. At the time they were looking like contenders for the Double. The 3–1 humbling at Dean Park did at least mean that Reynolds got a fresh opportunity in the first team. It was a short-lived return to the colours, though, because on Good Friday, 19 April, he was flattened by an opposing forward at Charlton Athletic and, much the worse for wear, saw out the rest of the game on the wing. The run-in, without Reynolds, would see Spurs finish as creditable runners-up.

A few weeks after Ron was clobbered Peter McParland thudded into Manchester United's goalie, Ray Wood, in the FA Cup Final, fracturing his cheekbone and leaving him a passenger on the wing, too. Villa won the game 2–1, but the outcry over Wood's injury – sustained in the glare of TV coverage – meant that keepers would finally receive a fairer deal from the game.

The debate as to what should be done raged up and down the country. One of the strongest advocates of greater protection was, ironically, a forward: West Bromwich Albion and England striker Ronnie Allen. Writing in the *FA News*, Allen said, 'Football is a game of skill and I often think that if we were to introduce this no-charging rule the goalkeepers of this country would improve generally. One of our goalkeepers, Norman Heath, had to quit his livelihood as a result of a charge by an onrushing centre-forward. Heath had collected the ball and the centre-forward charged as the law permits. Unfortunately, it affected the goalkeeper's spine, resulting in permanent injury.' Allen's support came as no surprise to Ron, who rated him highly: 'Ronnie was one of the most intelligent men I came across, and he was another devotee of the coaching sessions at Lilleshall. We always had great games against one another – one of the best of my career was at The Hawthorns when we drew 1–1 and Ronnie got a late equaliser.'

In addition to Allen's defence of the man at the back, FA staff coach Trevor Churchill, himself a former custodian, threw his weight behind moves to change the laws: 'I suffered two serious injuries as a goalkeeper. One resulted in fractured ribs caused by an opponent shoulder charging heavily whilst I was off the ground and making a high catch. The other was a fractured collar bone sustained after a save had been made, by an opponent following through and with no chance of getting the ball. The interesting point about both of these injuries was that the referee didn't even award a free-kick or administer a caution.' Adding that an immediate change in the keepers' favour was unlikely, Churchill added, 'Many goalkeepers would do well to take a supervised course in weight exercising and ally this to their normal training; this would ensure a physique tough enough to withstand the most vigorous legitimate charge.' Good advice given the climate perhaps, but hardly comforting.

Further calls for change came from Birmingham and England keeper Gil Merrick, who was quick to dismiss any suggestions that goalies were going soft: 'The fellow in the green jersey is usually a tall and strong sort of chap who has no wish to be wrapped up in cotton-wool. In fact he is normally the kind who relishes a challenge. But I am convinced that charging is needless and liable only to lead to trouble.'

Oddly, though, some of the most vociferous calls to leave well alone came from within the goalkeeping fraternity itself, including the Bournemouth and Boscombe Athletic number 1, Thomas Goodwin, who opined that it was quite right for forwards to chase the ball, 'as it runs towards the goalkeeper if there is a 50–50 chance of scoring or obtaining possession, even though such a chance frequently ends up in a collision. With practice, however, a goalie can learn to fall on the ball in such a way that he will seldom get badly hurt. I find that this type of charging keeps a goalkeeper fully on the alert for the whole 90 minutes.' In which case, the odd fractured cheekbone or broken spine was well worth it, presumably.

For the families left at home, though, it was often like being on a war watch, waiting for bad news from the front, as David Reynolds remembers: 'I can recall on many occasions waiting up because we'd had a phone call to say that he'd been injured and that he was in hospital somewhere. You never knew whether he was coming home that night or whether he was going to stay in hospital, and it was invariably a fracture or concussion. Dad used to put his head in where others feared to tread and he wasn't the only one – everybody remembers what happened to Bert Trautmann when he broke his neck in that FA Cup Final in 1956, but it wasn't an isolated thing. The centre-forward's job was to whack the goalkeeper and, to be fair, whenever Dad did get hurt, Tottenham couldn't really complain because they had one of the best exponents of that style in Bobby Smith. He was a big, bruising, old-fashioned centre-forward. You came up against that week in, week out and the injuries would mount up.

'I don't suppose the injuries were treated that well either, judging by the number of old players who are hobbling around in a bit of a state these days. Most of them would play when they really weren't fit enough because, on the money they were on, you didn't dare lose your place in the team and the chance of getting a win bonus. That was a big slice of their income and they couldn't risk losing it, so they'd go out and play with bandages and strappings on and then later on they'd play with painkilling injections. None of it did them any good in the long term and you read about so many of them having hips replaced or crippled with arthritis as a result. But in those days, you had to play or your living was at risk.'

Tottenham seemed to have turned the corner under Anderson, and the next season, 1957/58, further reinforced that view, at least as far as the league table was concerned. Spurs were again in the upper echelons of the First Division, ultimately ending the season in a solid third place, but that was a position that masked continuing weaknesses within the side. And, all the more frustrating for Ron, he spent plenty of the year on the sidelines looking on. At least that gave him a chance to observe the work of Jimmy Anderson at close quarters. Put simply, he remained stoically unimpressed: 'Anderson was never a manager who mixed with the players, not a "tracksuit" manager, as they were known later. He stuck pretty much to his office and from there he'd pick the team and decide on the way we were going to play without ever really getting involved on the training field or with the players themselves, which upset quite a few of us. Arthur Rowe had relied heavily on his staff to take training, but

Spurs' first-team squad lounging around on the deck of the Empress of England *and on land in Canada, May 1957; (bottom) with Ron Henry, Bobby Smith and Terry Medwin in Canada*

he was always there and among the players, and so we responded to him. With Anderson, it was clear that his main concern was to stay on good terms with the directors and never mind the players, which didn't go down well.

'So Bill Nicholson used to take the training, and because he'd been brought up under push and run and with Arthur's methods, there wasn't a great deal of difference. When Anderson *did* get involved, it was generally to make things worse. He brought in one individual who had been coaching on the continent, mainly in Italy, for some years, and he asked him to come and work with us alongside Bill. Well, it was crazy, farcical. He introduced this ridiculous system, a mad scheme whereby for several weeks he invited schoolboys from a local school to come and train with us. It wasn't a question of letting the local kids come and watch us train and then get some autographs: he had them playing, youngsters in among us in five-a-side games! With all due respect, this was absolutely ludicrous. When footballers are training, they should be at work, not messing about, they have a job to do. But when you're playing with and against children, then of course you can't do things properly, you have to worry about them getting hurt and all these kinds of things. Though, as it turned out, that was the last thing I needed to worry about.

'For some unknown reason, all goalkeepers like to play out in the field when it comes to five a side. On one occasion, when the children were playing with us, I finished up receiving a kick on the shin from one of these youngsters. You could see the blessed lump that came up on my leg. The boys were just overexcited and in the end it wasn't a disaster, but just imagine if they'd put Danny Blanchflower or Terry Medwin out of action for a couple of weeks.

'That was just one example of where Anderson wasn't really in touch with things. He'd simply been seduced by the fact that this coach had had success in Italy and must therefore be a good coach to have in England without ever looking into his methods to see if they were applicable to us. It was left to Bill Nicholson, a very good coach, to see him off and restore things to the way they had been under Arthur. That's one of the main reasons why results began to improve under Anderson, for a time at least.'

The Empire State Building. Ron was quite taken with America.

At the end of the 1957/58 season, Jimmy Anderson's best days as Tottenham manager were already well behind him. The drive towards immortality would have to go on without him. But would Ron Reynolds be a casualty, too?

CHAPTER FOURTEEN

One of the keys to Tottenham's revival in the mid-1950s was the form and intelligence of Robert Dennis Blanchflower. Danny, as he was known, took the Footballer of the Year award for the 1957/58 season, due reward for a player who took the phrase 'the beautiful game' literally, and did his utmost to turn football into an intellectual pursuit. In some respects, Blanchflower was playing at pretty much the perfect club to reflect and nurture those tastes, because the Spurs of yore, of Arthur Rowe and push and run, was almost a footballing university, certainly a debating society, where ideas about the game, about players, oppositions and tactics were the currency of conversation.

That remained a part of Tottenham life, though less so under Jimmy Anderson, with Ron Reynolds remembering, 'It was a far less lively dressing room, and there wasn't so much thought put into the game as there had been when I first joined the club. It was Bill Nicholson who redressed that to some extent, but really Danny was the ringleader. He was the one who would do nothing but talk about football, would act as the devil's advocate just to get the dressing room going and to get everyone involved. Danny wanted everybody to be fit in the mind as well as in body.

'Everybody took to Danny; everybody apart from some of the management, because they couldn't understand him and the things that he wanted to do, and I think they were probably a bit afraid of him, too. Things went well for a time, but when the changes at the top were made once Arthur had gone, it was obvious that Danny wasn't going to get away with it. His ideas were too far ahead of the times. His knowledge and vision were fantastic.'

Ron struck up a firm and enduring friendship with Blanchflower, for both were from the same school and of the same mind. Ron's regular visits to Lilleshall to soak up the latest coaching lessons kept him at the forefront of the coaching revolution, as well as helping him earn a few extra shillings, not least by penning an instructional column in the pages of the boys' comic *The Eagle*, in which he advised the footballers of the future on every aspect of the game. Even as late as 1958 this was still valuable income, because his total earnings from Spurs for the tax year to April was just over £943, on which he paid £98 in tax; £23 were added by coaching sessions for the Football Association.

On other occasions, Danny Blanchflower helped Ron augment his meagre income, as Ron recalled: 'Danny was an intelligent fellow and it was no surprise that he was very much sought-after to write newspaper columns and the like, and he was quickly under contract to the *Daily Express*. Because of that, he couldn't write for anyone else, but he always knew if any of the press needed an article. In that good cup run back in 1955/56 we were up against West Ham and drew with them at White Hart Lane. The replay was in the following midweek over at Upton Park and as we were travelling down there, Danny turned to me and said, "Would you like to do an article for one of the papers? I'm under contract to the *Express* and I can't do it." So I said, "Fair enough." He said, "After the game has finished, we'll be taken by car over to Fleet Street. I'll come over there with you and we'll do the article together."'

'After the game, we did the article together. I would say it was ninety-nine per cent Danny Blanchflower and one per cent Ron Reynolds, and when I got the cheque, because the article was under my name, I said to Danny, "There's no way I'm going to take this. I'll take just enough to cover my time."

'He refused: he wouldn't take a penny. He didn't have to do that. He wasn't earning sufficient in those days, even with whatever he was getting from the *Express* – none of us were. So, to me, that really illustrates what a magnificent fellow this man was. All the way through in the time that I knew him he was an idol as far as I was concerned.'

Money, even on the small scale that was received for a newspaper article, really did count in the late 1950s, with players still hidebound by the maximum wage. And in Ron's case, these paltry sums were for a man who was very much on the mind of England boss Walter Winterbottom when he came to select his squad for the 1958 World Cup. Ron was certainly in the running to make the trip, but the late-season injury he suffered against Charlton, coupled with England's decision to take just two keepers with them to Sweden, ultimately ruled him out, a situation he accepted phlegmatically: 'It was only later that I learned from Walter that I might have had a chance of going to the World Cup. That would have been a very valuable experience, not just as a player but as an observer, to see how Walter worked with our players at close hand and to see the other countries taking part in the competition. At the time, I didn't realise I was so close to getting a place in the squad. I was more concerned with the fact that, because of injury, I couldn't really hold down a regular place at Tottenham. Because of the problems I had there, I never had any great thoughts about breaking into the England set-up.'

While Reynolds was left behind, Blanchflower travelled out to Sweden as the Northern Irish qualified for the final phase of the World Cup for the first time. Once out there, Danny showed himself to be a pivotal figure for a side that fared far better than their lowly status as minnows had ever suggested. 'Danny was the kind of player who played better and better the higher the level,' Ron remembered. 'He was a slow mover, but it all went on in his head – the way people talk about the likes of Cantona or Sheringham, a thinking footballer – and that more than compensated for his lack of pace. When he eventually teamed up with Dave Mackay, he was allowed to have the same impact at Spurs that Cantona did with Roy Keane behind him at Manchester United. Because at international level the game tended to be slower than it was in England at that time, when it was still very much kick and rush from a lot of teams, because you had more time on the ball, Danny came into his own.'

Over the years the two were together at Spurs, Reynolds and Blanchflower became co-conspirators, always discussing football, unafraid to go off at tangents in the hope it might lead them to some better understanding or appreciation of another facet of the game, always seeking new and different ways of thinking, preparing and playing. Yet the two had very different approaches. Ron would immerse himself in coaching courses at Lilleshall, while Blanch-flower would try to feed his mind simply by thinking and watching others play – not for him the strictures of coaching badges, as Ron remembered: 'I don't think Danny ever took to being told anything. He wasn't a great one for rules and regulations or for listening to the handed-down ways of doing things. He was always somebody who wanted to find things out for himself. That's not to say he was blinkered, because he wasn't, but he would always prefer to come up with an idea and then test it to see if it worked, rather than being given instruction.

'And he was a great talker: he always wanted to talk because he felt that was the best way of learning. He enjoyed conversations because he thought if two or more people were putting in ideas, you had a better chance of coming up with better solutions than you did by simply going into a classroom and having an instructor or a coach tell you what to do. That was a good approach and it didn't do him any harm, but equally I think that by going to Lilleshall myself and by seeing what the new thinking there was, from talking to other players and coaches, I got a wider view than Danny did. He always pumped me for information when I returned from Lilleshall anyway, so he must have felt that there was something going on there that was worth knowing about.'

Ironically, it was Blanchflower who went into print with a book which dealt with coaching, as well as the rest of his life in football, rather than the more qualified Reynolds – an early indication that football was increasingly about big names as much as it was about substance. Blanchflower's book was well received, commended for being not just elegantly written, as expected, but technically sound. That surprised many critics, but the credit didn't necessarily go in the right direction. Much of Danny's spade work was done by Ron Reynolds.

'I probably got on with Danny more than anybody, although I didn't live locally, which meant that I didn't see Danny in "off" moments, as it were. Our conversations were mainly in the dressing room before and after training. If we went away – special training before big games, that sort of thing – we got on very well because our beliefs were very similar. Danny believed in stylish football. We talked the same game. In those days I was a senior coach on the FA Panel and we wanted to take the game forward. I think I'm right in saying I was the only qualified coach at White Hart Lane. We were both preaching to the converted when we talked to each other, and we used to chat about the game in our spare moments. When he wrote his book, he would draft out certain sections and on many occasions would hand me these sheets and say, "Have a look through that and see what you think, and if you have any comments to make – make them." We went on a close-season tour to Hungary and I spent all of my spare time looking at these blessed sheets. He specifically wanted to know what I thought about his points on coaching, so I had a fair bit of technical input on that.

'Danny had a lot of good ideas, very original ideas, but, being Danny, he had a very individual way of putting them over, which made them more difficult to understand for the lay person. Danny would try to convey his ideas in an almost philosophical fashion and he would use the sort of prose that you would find him using in newspaper columns. So I helped him pare it back a little, to get down to the nub of what he was saying, to give it a more "technical" element, I suppose, using diagrams to get points across more easily, for example.'

Coaching was becoming the hot topic of the time, as England continued to fail to make an impact on the international scene, notably in World Cup tournaments. The Players' Union was despairing of the national side's failure in the national game, and wrote an impassioned plea to the Football Association, calling on the game's establishment to turn the tide, at school level at the very least: 'The present FA coaching sessions consist of six one-hour or two three-hour lessons. How can anyone hope to cover the vast area that football demands in six hours? Ought we not really to get down to teaching the game thoroughly? Instead of letting coaches struggle with boys who have absolutely no interest in the game, weed them out and give the lads who wish to learn all the time and attention of the coach. Why not attach a coach to a school for a full season? If cost should be the main obstacle, then we feel that ways and means of raising the necessary finance can and must be found for this essential step forward.'

But the Players' Union didn't turn its fire solely on the Football Association. It also insisted that its own members do everything in their own power to raise the standard of football in this country, adding, 'There can be no room for those who consider they know all there is to know and are not prepared to keep on learning.' In spite of the inconsistencies of recent years, and the changing approach under Jimmy Anderson, Tottenham had been, and remained, a club where the players did their utmost to continue learning and improving. In the main they did this by bringing fresh talent in from outside, rather than promoting the reserves.

Going into the 1958/59 season they paid £35,000, a record for a winger, to Swansea for the services of Cliff Jones, who had been a sensation for Wales in the 1958 World Cup, despite never having trained full time before his move to London. Circumstances there might have suggested that he'd have been better off staying part time, given the appalling mishap that befell him in pre-season training, a day that Ron Reynolds remembered vividly: 'We did all of our work in pre-season up at the training ground in Cheshunt, that was our normal routine. We'd start for the first week by doing just fitness work to get over the rustiness and then we'd get down to proper work with the ball after

*Experimental use of photography to include those who couldn't
make it for the photocall for the 1958 team shot*

that. It was a couple of weeks into the pre-season and on this particular day we ended the session with a full-scale practice match, with the
first-team forwards and reserve defenders playing against the reserve-
team forwards and first-team defenders.

'The game hadn't been going on all that long when there was a
hell of a crack. Peter Baker had gone in to tackle Cliff Jones, who
was so fast, and he caught him and broke his leg. That was the beginning of August 1958, a couple of weeks away from the start of the
season, and we'd lost our new signing, probably for the entire season.
You can imagine, we were all very downcast after that and the
session ended pretty much straight away. We all trooped off home
while Cliff was taken to hospital.

'So I drove back to Haslemere from Cheshunt, and it was a nasty
drive because it had been pouring with rain during the day. I got
home and parked the car outside. I went in, had a meal and said to
my wife "I'm going out now to put the car away." So I drove the car
into the garage, opened the door into the side of the garage. But the

*(Anti-clockwise from bottom right) August 1958. Pre-season photo shoot (*News of the World*).*
The wife, the kids, the garage door . . .

door swung back on my finger. I looked down and I had just sliced off the end of a finger!

'So in the morning we lost Cliff Jones to a broken leg for the whole season, and then I had to phone Jimmy Anderson and tell him that I wouldn't be playing for some time. That was two first-teamers out of action for the start of the new season. It was especially galling for me because I felt I'd seen off Ted Ditchburn at last and was going to make myself the number-one goalkeeper, the first choice. Oddly enough, Ted then got injured as well, and it was Johnny Hollowbread who came into the side and pretty much took over after he'd had something like six years at the club just waiting for his first chance to play.'

Ron's son David was at home when his dad suffered what would be a nasty accident for anybody, but one which was potentially devastating for a goalkeeper: ' I can remember him coming in and saying, "I think I've lost the top off my finger," and there it was in his other hand. So he got whisked off to hospital and that was a bit of a worrying time. I know my mother was worried because she thought his career could be up the spout. Luckily, it didn't affect his goalkeeping too much, because he still had most of his finger left.'

Ron's rehabilitation was so quick that by early October he was back in harness again, making a comeback in the Spurs reserves side that played a friendly at Cambridge on a Thursday afternoon, a game which Ron came through completely unscathed: 'I was delighted to get through the game because, of course, I was concerned that a hand injury might be too difficult to deal with. So I was very pleased, and on the Friday morning, I sent a letter to the surgeon who had done the job on the finger, thanking him for what he'd done and confirming I'd started back again and had come through the first game successfully.

'The next Monday night, we had a game against Queen's Park Rangers at White Hart Lane, and this one was under the floodlights. Ronnie Henry passed a suicidal ball back to me and I had to go down for it, right at the forward's feet. I had some protection on that finger, but the QPR forward came in and *bang*! He caught me at the end of that finger.

36(a). Top: *J. Carver, formerly a player with Blackburn Rovers during the 1930s, went to the continent on retirement from playing and became a world-famous coach. He is seen here coaching players of Tottenham Hotspur, 1958.*

'So on the Tuesday morning, I finished up back in hospital. The surgeon walks in and says, "Thank you very much for the kind letter, I've just been reading it. I'm so pleased that you appreciated it. Now, what the hell are you in here for?" I was out of action again for about another four weeks.'

While Reynolds and Jones were stuck on the sidelines, their playing colleagues were struggling at the bottom of the First Division, though Ron conceded that his replacement, Johnny Hollowbread, was 'doing very well, considering he had never had a first-team game in his life before'. But Spurs had had a disastrous opening that saw them leave August without a point on the board after losing at home to Blackpool and getting thumped at Chelsea and Blackburn. September looked a little brighter, but the writing was on the wall, and in early October the Spurs board decided that it was time for action, as Ron remembered: 'The change had been coming ever since Arthur left. Anderson didn't last long as a manager – and there was never any opportunity for him to last long as a manager because everybody saw through him. They had to do something about it. They had to rectify a very bad situation and Bill

Nicholson was the obvious answer. He stepped up from being coach to managing the side, and the results spoke for themselves after that.' The first result didn't so much speak as scream, with Tottenham taking Everton to the cleaners, winning 10–4. Blanchflower told Bill Nicholson afterwards, 'I hope you won't be expecting us to do that every week!'

Nicholson didn't expect it from Blanchflower personally, that's for sure, because within weeks he was joining Reynolds in the reserve team, as Nicholson branded him an 'expensive luxury' in a team that was fighting for survival. The fact that Tottenham ultimately stabilised and pulled away from the bottom, eventually surviving by six points, suggests there was some merit in Nicholson's decision, but his handling of the incumbent Footballer of the Year suggested that he had a lot to learn about man management.

As Ron was about to discover.

CHAPTER FIFTEEN

Ron, Danny and flowers in Kiev, May 1959

Although goalkeepers generally enjoy greater longevity than their outfield counterparts, even they begin to feel the cold breath of their own mortality when they enter their thirties, when they begin to realise that their time as players is running out. Perhaps things are different now, with football awash with cash, but in the maximum-wage era being a footballer was less about amassing an investment portfolio and more about getting on the field and playing some games, making your mark on the history of the game, and sharing in its joy and glory.

Ron Reynolds had spent more than his fair share of time on the sidelines at Spurs, initially honing his trade in the shadow of Ted Ditchburn and then, once he'd overtaken him in the pecking order, being forced to spend weeks consigned to the treatment room, fighting off a whole host of injuries. Rarely since he'd left Aldershot could he have said that he was the undisputed number 1 at White Hart Lane.

Much would have been different had it not been for that nasty car accident at the beginning of the 1958/59 season. With Ditchburn in his dotage and Johnny Hollowbread definitely third in line, that would surely have been when the now thirty-year-old Reynolds came of age and made the number 1 shirt all his own. Instead, he found himself back on the sidelines, holding a watching brief, struggling back to full health and fitness as another season drifted by.

There was never any suggestion that Spurs were looking to get rid of Ron however, and when the retained list came out in the summer of 1959 his name was on it once again, alongside Hollowbread's. That fact alone was enough to give Ron fresh hope that he might be first choice in goal, especially after what had been another tough season for Tottenham, when they'd come eighteenth and conceded a massive ninety-five goals. Clearly, new manager Bill Nicholson would be looking to make some improvements to the team, not least defensively.

That impression had been reinforced during the latter stages of the 1958/59 season when, with Spurs finally safe from the relegation battle, Nicholson had sought out Reynolds for a one-to-one chat about the future. According to Ron, 'We were about three or four weeks away from the end of the season and after training Bill Nick told me that he wanted to see me in his office immediately. I was still in the reserves at that point, and I thought that I was playing well enough, but probably not spectacularly enough to displace Johnny, because he was playing quite well too, despite the results we were getting. He certainly wasn't having a terrible time personally or anything like that, and in those circumstances it's unlikely that the manager will change the goalkeeper.

'So I wasn't really sure what it was that Bill wanted to see me about. Though, with the season coming towards a close, I wondered if it might have something to do with the retained list, or even that another club had made an enquiry about me. When I heard what it was that he had to tell me, I was very surprised. He said, "I don't want you to say anything to anybody at all about this, but I'm taking you to Russia with us for our tour there when the season is finished, and I want to tell you that you are not going to be going just to be

The two great team-mates on their way to Russia

our reserve goalkeeper this time. But I have to tell you again that I don't want you to say anything to anybody about any of this. It's got to be a surprise to you when you see the names go up on the team sheets when we get there. We've got three games over there and I'll be playing you in two of the games, although Johnny will probably play in the first of the three."

'I was rather taken aback by it all, but I thought that was an indication he was willing to let me have a go after all the injury problems I'd had during that season. So we went over there and, to give him credit, Bill was as good as his word about the whole thing. Johnny Hollowbread played in Moscow in the first game, which was a draw, but after that Bill changed the side and put me in goal in the game we played against Kiev. It was a hard match, but we won 0–1 and I thought I'd played my part by keeping out the opposition. Bill seemed very pleased and at the end of the game he congratulated me. He said, "Great, I'm glad you managed to do it, keep it going."'

'After that we went to Leningrad, which for me was the most important game, to see if Bill would keep his word and let me play again. I was rather relieved when I saw the team and I was still in it, because it seemed to prove to me that I did have a future at Tottenham, and that I could look ahead to playing regularly the next

Prior to the match in Kiev

season. The match itself was very interesting because we were up against the national side, and the game took place at midnight. It was all open air: I don't think there was a covered stand in the ground, but it was the national stadium. They were a very strong side, as you would expect, but we didn't do badly and lost 1–3, with the third goal coming from a penalty that Dave Mackay gave away, so we'd pushed them very hard throughout the game.

'Again Bill Nicholson made a point of congratulating me afterwards, and Danny Blanchflower was absolutely thrilled for me. These were my first games for over a year, so Danny was just bubbling over for me. You can just imagine how pleased he was to be there at the time when Nicholson congratulated me on the tour. Danny said, "Following this, keep it quiet, but next season you're in."

'Personally, I was just pleased to be back in the first team again and to have done myself justice in a couple of difficult games for the club, and it meant that I could come home to the family, enjoy a few weeks' break before pre-season training and look forward to playing regularly in the first team again. That was the biggest thing. After missing an entire season, and with me coming up to my thirty-first birthday, what mattered most was to get back into the first team and play football. Otherwise, what was the point of being a footballer?'

Clearly, playing mattered more than anything to Ron, but, equally, he appreciated the peripheral perks that came with the job, especially the opportunity it gave him to explore the world, as his son David remembers: 'He did travel quite a lot with Spurs. I think that to a certain extent they were one of the great pioneering teams from England, who made a point of going off into Europe. They went to Russia, Holland, Germany, Denmark. They were one of the prime movers behind what is now the UEFA Cup, which started out as the old Inter Cities Fairs Cup, where teams from European cities met each other in a cup competition. There was a London combination team to start with in that, and Dad represented them in a couple of games and he got to play in Barcelona as part of that. I know he loved that, the opportunity to go and see new places.

'It was all uncharted territory for them, especially going to

It's unlikely that today's Spurs first-team squad would stroll around Red Square smoking Rothman's

Russia, behind the Iron Curtain, and I think some of the players were at a loss as to how to behave. When they were out there, obviously the country was very poor, there were no souvenir shops for them to bring things home for their families. In Russia, one of the players put a couple of spoons from the hotel in his pocket to bring back home with him as a souvenir, and he was immediately swooped upon. They almost had a diplomatic incident on their hands. I remember Dad telling us that the management had had to work overtime to stop the authorities carting this player off to Siberia!

'Dad just brought home these little packets of sugar from one of the hotels that they'd stayed in, because it had the name of the hotel on it in Russian, so that was a novelty. When we took the sugar out, it was a horrible, dirty colour, not very appetising.'

David also recalls his dad making friends abroad: 'I remember they played in Switzerland once or twice and he got friendly with a hotelier out there. We got a decent holiday out of that, in Basle, when I was a kid. So, even then, football opened doors for you: you met people from all walks of life and there were benefits from that. The other side was the hangers on: he was always getting calls for tickets and had to differentiate between the genuine and the others. He was very good at that, even up to the time he died. A chap called him up, a Spurs fan who had terminal cancer, and he asked Dad if he could get him tickets for a Tottenham–Chelsea game. Even though Dad's connections were pretty much severed, he called the club and managed to get some really good tickets sorted out. He used to do things like that when we were in business, too: he'd put himself out for little old ladies who were befuddled by the Inland Revenue. That was how he was.'

Others, especially in the cut-throat world of football, were not as kind, so perhaps Ron shouldn't have been surprised when Bill Nicholson's promises proved to be empty ones, just days after they were made. 'We got back from Russia and we had a month or so before we all got back together again for our pre-season training at Tottenham,' recalled Ron. 'So all the boys headed off on holiday with their families. We went to Paignton – these were the days before people went abroad on holiday. Anyway, I picked up a newspaper one morning and read it over breakfast. Like everybody else, I turned to the back pages first and opened it up at the football news and there it was: "Bill Nicholson buys Bill Brown from Dundee". Apparently Nicholson felt that we needed a new goalkeeper to replace Ted Ditchburn and he'd brought Bill in to play in the first team.

'Well, that was it as far as I was concerned. I had no qualms about Bill Brown as a goalkeeper, nor as a man, but not three weeks before he signed Nicholson had been telling me that I would be his first choice in the new season, telling me what a great job I'd done in Russia and that my place was safe at Tottenham. Then he went out and bought another goalkeeper to replace both myself and Johnny Hollowbread.

'Nobody in football is immune to having their place taken from them: we all take that as an occupational hazard, it's something that happens. You accept that. But what I couldn't accept was that I had been told I would be in the first team one minute and then I'd had that taken away from me, without even having played any games in the interim.

'As soon as we got back for pre-season training, I went straight in to see Bill Nicholson and I told him what I thought of the situation and that I wanted to leave the club as soon as I possibly could. It was an intolerable situation to be in. I had no respect left for him after what he had done, especially as when I did get in to see him, he said that it hadn't been anything to do with him, that he'd been told to buy a new goalkeeper by the board. He shifted the onus on to them, trying to divert the blame away from himself. That meant I had even less respect for him.

'Danny Blanchflower did try to smooth things over and told me not to stick my neck out, it would all come right in the end, but I felt let down by it all. That was Danny's way, and perhaps he was right, because although he had a go at authority, he could get away with it. He was sort of tongue in cheek and was never abrasive. He was sufficiently aware of how far he could go, whereas I wasn't concerned with that. He had a knack of getting away with things, because he was soft spoken and everybody tends to have a picture in their mind of him as this laughing, joking Irishman. I think we had a board of directors at the time who wouldn't have known when they were being insulted, to be honest. We used to go away on trips and on the way back we used to insult them. I never knew a director at matches who'd put his hand in his pocket for a drink for the lads. Never once. We used to be so pointed with it and it was just like water off a duck's back – they never used to take any offence. Danny got away with it because the board were so weak from that point of view. But it was easier for him because at least he had some respect for Bill Nicholson, which I'd lost by the end.'

Ron's refusal to suffer fools or to accept what he saw as insulting behaviour meant there was no likelihood of any rapprochement with Nicholson, as David Reynolds accepts: 'Tottenham was a long period of his career, ten years or so, and I don't think he ever quite fully realised his potential there. I don't think he saw eye to eye with the hierarchy there. He had great respect for Arthur Rowe, but he never got on with Bill Nicholson. It was just one of those situations where Nicholson picked the side and a lot of the time, for one reason or another, Dad wasn't in it. He had a few barneys there, because he'd have a barney with anyone. If he thought there was something wrong, he'd say so: he called a spade a spade and I think he made enemies that way. On the other hand, people respected him because he wouldn't just kow-tow to authority. He was very argumentative because he always thought he was in the right. It's hard to see how he and Blanchflower got on because they were both very stubborn. But they got on well – they probably liked having someone to argue with!'

The arrival of Bill Brown wasn't the end of the indignities heaped upon Ron, in what turned out to be a very unhappy final nine months at White Hart Lane, as he recalled: 'A couple of weeks after I'd asked for a transfer, we started to play some friendlies, and, of course, Bill was in goal. Now, after a few of these games, and just a few weeks after he'd bought an expensive new goalkeeper to replace me, Bill Nicholson came up to me in the middle of training and said, "Ron, in our matches so far, Bill's flapping at every ball that comes across into the area. He doesn't catch the ball, he just flaps at it. So for the next part of the session, I want you to take him with you. Go up to the goal and take young Barry Atchison [a reserve outside-right] with you and I want you to coach Bill on how to catch every kind of cross that can come in." You can imagine what I felt about that: I wasn't good enough to be in the side but I was good enough to teach the man who replaced me how to do the job properly. I couldn't believe it. Anyway, I did it. I suppose Bill would say, "You're a fully qualified coach, who else did I have?" But it was a ridiculous situation, and not just for me: it was obviously very awkward for Bill Brown, too.'

Brown, like the whole Spurs side, improved dramatically, and the team finished third in Division One in 1959/60, just two points behind the champions, Burnley. To achieve that level of success for the first team, Nicholson and his small staff had little interest in other matters. That put himself on the wrong side of Ron yet again: 'Just before the opening match of the season, at the end of training, Bill got in touch with me and Johnny Hollowbread and said, "I want to see you both in my office." This was probably on the Thursday because the team sheet usually went up on the Friday. We both got inside his office and he said, "Now, you know the situation here: Bill's in the first team, you two are in the reserves, but I want you both to have regular match practice so that if you need to come into the first team, you'll be ready. I've got plenty to worry about with looking after the first team, so I don't want to have to think about selecting which one of you plays in the reserves, so you'll play alternately. One of you will play one week and the other will play the next in the reserves, so you can pick and choose which games you play." And he left it to Johnny Hollowbread and myself!"

'I said, "Bill, if we do that, one is going to get all the home games and the other will end up with all away games.' He just turned round and said, "If you want to play two weeks running and then the other plays for two weeks running, then just you please yourselves. Do what you like."

'From a manager, this was diabolical. What respect did he get from me? What respect did he get from Johnny Hollowbread? I couldn't wait to get away from the place.'

But Ron found himself consigned to the 'one week on, one week off' rota for much of the 1959/60 season. He remained in the dark as to whether anyone came in for him during that period, or whether Spurs simply didn't want to sell and were dismissing any offers out of hand. Finally, though, blessed relief came by way of a call from an old friend on the south coast, as Ron remembered: 'I'd resigned myself to seeing out the season at Tottenham because it was March 1960 and I was still there. It was the day before the transfer deadline, when suddenly Bill Nicholson came over to me in training and said, "I want to see you afterwards." So I went to the office and he said, "Do you fancy a move to Southampton?" I asked him if Ted Bates, who was manager there, had been on to him, because I knew Ted pretty well from visits to Lilleshall. We were both regulars up there.

'Bill told me that Ted was interested in signing me for Southampton, so I told him, "You get on the phone to Ted and tell him that I'll get down there as soon as I can this afternoon and that, if he wants, I'll sign for him there and then." Instead of going home, I drove straight down to Southampton from Cheshunt, which was a heck of a drive at the best of times, but the transfer deadline was looming and I wasn't going to miss out on the opportunity. Ted never had an easier signing to make – never. Within half an hour I'd signed. Over a cup of tea in the Polygon Hotel in the centre of Southampton.

'I'd had ten good years at Tottenham, but it had gone very sour towards the end. I wasn't playing any football, there was no hope of me playing any, so it was time to move on and Southampton was ideal for me. It was a shame because Spurs had a very good side by then: the younger players had got experience and it was obvious that they would go on to great things. As they did the next year, of course, when they won the Double. It would have been nice to have been part of that and to be with my friends there but I would have been only a bit-part player at best, so it was time to go. I'd asked Danny whether I should go to Southampton and he'd said, "Well, you know your days here are numbered." So off I went.

'I didn't see Danny or the boys much after that, until I was at a TV show in the Southern TV studios with the rest of the Southampton team, and Danny was on as well. Before the show started, we had time for a bit of a chat, and Danny said to me, "Well, it may not be any good for you to know this now, Ron, but it may do your ego a bit of good. When you were transferred down here, you were the best goalkeeper of the three that we had at Tottenham. And that comes from Nicholson himself!'

In spite of that, Ron would never get another chance to prove his class, not in the First Division at least. Instead, he headed off for The Dell, to pick up his career in the Third Division.

SOUTHAMPTON

CHAPTER SIXTEEN

When Ron made the move to Southampton in 1960, it was to join a team that was doing just as well in its division as Spurs had been doing in theirs, with the Saints on the verge of promotion to Division Two. Without a doubt, Southampton had been one of the beneficiaries of the reorganisation of the Football League which had taken place two seasons previously. At the end of 1957/58, the regionalised Third Division was abolished and for the next season nationwide Third and Fourth Divisions were installed in its place, giving clubs a far better grasp of their exact position in the league pyramid, and, many felt, a better chance of progress.

Under the old Third Division North and South set-up, only one club from each league could secure promotion into the Second Division. With only the champions winning promotion, in a year of a runaway leader interest in the season could be virtually over in February. Similarly, the second team in the North could be vastly superior to the leaders in the South, and yet be denied its rightful place in the higher league. Add to that the annual debates about whether North was generally stronger than the South, and which division the likes of Port Vale and Walsall should be in, and you had a system that was reaching the end of its useful life. The burgeoning road network, which made long-distance travel easier, was the clinching argument: the concept has endured until today, although in the light of the ITV Digital disaster, the possibility of its imminent return should not be discounted.

In the latter stages of regionalisation the Saints had struggled to mount a serious challenge in the Third Division South. Since relegation from Division Two in 1952/53, they'd come sixth, third, fourteenth, fourth and sixth: usually solid enough, but never threatening to win promotion. The structural changes brought real hope of progress, notwithstanding the fact that the competition would be stiffer, given the influx of half a division's worth of northern outfits.

The 1958/59 season saw them struggling to find their feet in this new league, finishing fourteenth after a year of toil. For 1959/60, Ted Bates saw where the problems lay and went about some drastic surgery, cutting fourteen players and bringing in nine new faces, including the Chelsea wing-half Cliff Huxford, who became the hub of the team, alongside emerging winger Terry Paine, who had made his debut in March 1957 as a seventeen-year-old and was now exhibiting the qualities that would ultimately take him into the England side.

Bates' changes soon bore fruit, with Derek Reeves and George O'Brien teaming up in attack to smash sixty-two goals between them in the season. After a sluggish start, Southampton took 13 points out of 14 in a September burst, then lost just 2 of 19 league games from mid-October to early March. They also made it to the fourth round of the FA Cup, thumping First Division Manchester City 1–5 at Maine Road en route.

The glorious run came to a crashing halt, though, when in the space of five days in March Southampton were hammered 5–1 at Newport County and then 4–1 at Coventry City. Unwilling to wait and see if this were simply a nervous blip or a symptom of something more malign, Bates acted at once, dumping the incumbent

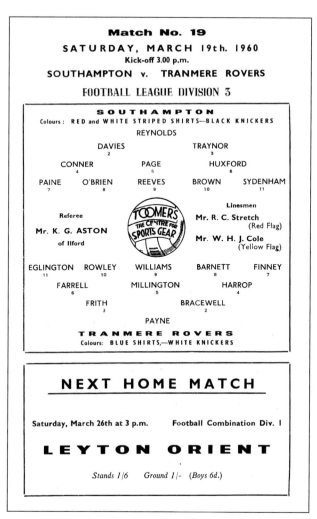

Ron takes his place immediately in the Saints' line-up against Tranmere Rovers

keeper Bob Charles and sending for Ron Reynolds, who joined on deadline day for £10,000.

He was straight into the first team, taking his place in goal in the 1–1 draw with Tranmere Rovers at The Dell. Having scored hatfuls of goals earlier in the season, the Saints now found themselves struggling in front of goal, but Ron's arrival meant that at least they weren't conceding. The rot was stopped as Southampton went on an unbeaten run of four games. Though three were draws, the ship was steadied and, with two promotion places up for grabs, they knew

*The presentation of the
trophy, and Skol-fuelled
celebration afterwards –
Southampton's Third
Division Championship,
May 1960 (*Sunday Mirror*)*

they were going up long before season's end. The championship was sealed on the final day of the season with a 2–0 win over Bradford City in front of 21,848 supporters at The Dell. For Ron, despite having arrived on the scene late in the day, it was the first time he had tasted real success with any of his three clubs.

'I was delighted that Ted asked me to go down to Southampton,' he recalled, 'because I knew him well and I knew he had similar views on the game to my own. He liked to play good football and I knew he was a good coach, so everything was there for me. Of course, I felt a little sorry for Bob Charles, who had been in goal before me, but at that stage of the season, they needed a bit more experience in there. Having been in front for so long, often the most difficult thing is to clinch the win. You see this in all sports, not just football, and so Ted thought he needed a player who had been involved in big games before and who wouldn't be put off his stride by them.

'It was very exciting to be involved in that run-in, especially as we had all but clinched promotion with quite a few games to go and were then just fighting for the championship, knowing that even if we missed out we were still going up. Having come from one of the top clubs in the country, it was very important to me that we won promotion. It was one of my happiest periods in football, playing a part in getting Southampton back into Division Two.'

As was mentioned earlier, one of the more appealing features of football forty years ago was the equality across the divisions. Nowadays, as soon as a team wins promotion, it's surrounded by gloomy prognoses about its chances in the higher league and the probability of its filling one of the following year's relegation slots. Back in 1960, as Southampton prepared for life in Division Two for the first time in seven years, they did so with some confidence. They'd been promoted by scoring goals as if it were going out of fashion, always a trait that gives a side hope that it can collect points wherever it goes. And, of course, they had shored up the defence with the arrival of Ron Reynolds. If promotion would not be on the agenda, a comfortable season away from the spectre of relegation, even a berth in the top half of the division, was a distinct possibility.

A hit with the press on the south coast

Certainly, Ron felt the Saints could go marching on to better things, not least because of the leadership of Ted Bates. He had been a former leader of the line as a player, making his Southampton debut on 27 December 1937 and going on to play in the same Southampton side as Alf Ramsey. Unlike Ramsey, who had very clear and fixed ideas and rarely felt the need to consult with other coaches, Bates, like Reynolds, was of the opinion that if English football were to progress, the pooling of ideas was critically important. He also felt that attendance at coaching seminars and sessions was an integral part of a learning process which was ongoing, another issue on which he and Ron agreed: 'Lilleshall was really where Ted and I got to know each other. Ted was never absent from those, always keen to get involved. We were pretty thick over the years, as I had been with Blanchflower at Spurs, though it was a little different because Danny was never so interested in the formal side of coaching. While I enjoyed my time at Tottenham, the best club I ever played for was under Ted Bates at Southampton. That was brilliant!'

In the new division Southampton settled down to business very well, winning four of the first six, including against neighbours Portsmouth, 5–1, and Liverpool, newly under the leadership of Bill Shankly, 4–1. Liverpool were also the victims in November when the two sides met in the third round of the first Football League Cup, setting up a fourth-round tie with Leeds. That early December tie was a manic occasion, with the game delayed for almost half an hour because the floodlights failed at The Dell. Reeves then put Southampton ahead just before Ron was carried off, injured and unable to resume. His friend Brian Pearce remembers the night vividly: 'When he moved to Southampton, he said to me that any time when I was free in midweek when Southampton had a match, if I could get along to Haslemere Station at four o'clock, he'd give me a lift to the game and bring me back to Guildford, which was very enjoyable.

'In the game against Leeds Ron was involved in a terrible collision with their centre-forward and he got concussion; broke a finger, too. As they rushed out to attend to poor Ron, the lights went out again, so they had to look after him in virtual darkness, lit by just the little stand lights.

'I was sitting at the front with the players' families, so I remember him being brought in front of us on a stretcher. Bob Charles, the reserve goalkeeper, was next to me and he nipped down to the dressing room to find out how Ron was. He came back and said, "They're taking him straight to hospital." I was concerned about Ron but, of course, I'd lost my lift, too, so I asked Bob if he knew when the next train back to Woking was. He said it was around nine o'clock, so I ran all the way to the station and just about made my train home.'

In spite of Ron's departure, ten-man Southampton went 4–0 up, all through Reeves, before Leeds put deputy goalkeeper Huxford under pressure, levelling the score at 4–4 before Reeves popped up again to grab his fifth moments before the final whistle.

Fortunately, this time around Ron missed just one game and was able to recapture his place in the first eleven as soon as he was fit again. It was a far cry from the days at Spurs when injury meant he'd be kicking his heels for weeks, even months. For Ron, this was a huge relief: 'People talk a lot about competition for places and having players who can come in and put pressure on those in the team, and there is something in that, but, equally, it can be destructive. If you are always looking over your shoulder, you're not always focused on your game and it can affect you. At Southampton, I knew I was first choice and that as long as I maintained my standards, I would keep that position, even if I missed games with injury. Perhaps it was because I was getting older, but I appreciated that and I'm sure that relaxed me and helped my game, and meant I played better as a result. The thing is that different ideas work for different players and good managers work out what you have to do for each one. Players are individuals, not machines.'

Certainly, Bates got the best out of his players, and, for much of the season, Southampton kept up with the pace-setters, notably Alf Ramsey's Ipswich. Much of that was down to Bates' tactical

(Opposite page) Ron in the sunshine at The Dell

acumen. Ron specifically remembered a cup tie against Ipswich: 'In the league we had gone to Portman Road and drawn with them, 3–3, but we were lucky to get away with it. Alf Ramsey had perfected a style of play that was virtually unseen in this country, very advanced tactically, and it staggered us when we saw it in action. It had the same impact on everybody else, too: they won the Second Division and then, the year after, went straight on and won the First!

'But we drew Ipswich at home in the FA Cup a couple of months later and needed to think about how we could combat them. There was a pre-match talk between the senior players, who were Tommy Traynor, Cliff Huxford, the skipper, who was left-half, and myself. We were called in by Ted Bates to have a word.

'He said, "You know what happened up there: they tore us to shreds." And he went through their tactics. It was a simple ploy that anything coming out of defence went through Jimmy Leadbetter, the left-winger. He moved back very deep, picking up balls and throw-outs from the goalkeeper, Roy Bailey. Balls out of defence inevitably found Leadbetter in a deep position and, regular as clockwork, he used to feed Ray Crawford, their number nine. Ray used to detach from the centre-forward position, come back and pick it up, lay it back, and then the through-ball went to Ted Phillips, the inside-left. Ted was very powerful and he could run with the ball, and with Ray dropping deep, he had room to run in to, because Ray would generally take the centre-half with him, to create all this space. Of course, Ted Bates was very anxious to blot this out. Unfortunately, although Dick Conner, our right-half, did well for us, he loved to get involved in the attacking play, and that was a problem because it meant he didn't really cover either Leadbetter or Phillips.

'Cliff Huxford was a great player and a great captain for the club. You've heard the expression many times about certain individuals, but literally if he had been playing against his grandmother, he'd have kicked her up in the stand! A very rugged, defensive player. So the suggestion was made to Cliff to switch to the right-half position. Cliff said, "Well, you know my strength is on the left-side, and if you tell Dick we're switching him because he can't look after Phillips, that's it, there'll be hell to pay."

'So I said, "Well, just kid him along. Suggest he'd be much better in a forward position where he hasn't got to worry about Phillips." Anyway, the suggestion was put to Dick in this way: "Would you like to switch so that you can forget the defensive duty?" Of course, Dick turned round and said, "Don't you think I can do the job, then? I'll show you what I can do!" And he did: we won 7–1! Everybody agrred that Dick played a great game: he was the man of the match.

'About three or four weeks afterwards, we were playing them at home in the league. Ted called the same three of us in and said, "What are we going to do now?" I said, "He's proved his point, he won't want to do it again. We're on a hiding to nothing if we tell him we're going to switch him." Dick was not the type of player who could be told what to do, even though he was a damn good player in his way.

'So Ted had a word with him, but it didn't do much good. We went out and Phillips should have had four in the first half, he had so much space. As it was, we got away with it again, and the game finished 1–1.'

For Ron, though, that wasn't the end of his association with Ipswich that season, as he recalled: 'After the game I ended up having a chat with Alf. I'll never forget this, because Alf was not the type of player you could converse with, so this was out of the ordinary. He was a very odd one, a loner. As I came out of our dressing room and approached the visitors' dressing room, Alf came out and he walked along with me, and it was as near to an invitation as any player could get to join them, which, of course, was completely illegal. He was tapping me up for a move to Ipswich without talking to Ted Bates or anybody else at Southampton. I think Alf was aware that Roy Bailey was going back home to South Africa. So he was full of questions, very solicitous, asking me, "How do you like it at Southampton? Are you enjoying your football down here? We would give you a lot more pleasure from the game. We could give you First Division football next season." In the end, I just told him, "Sorry, Alf, I'm happy where I am."'

The excellent draw with leaders Ipswich marked the end of Southampton's impressive run in the Second Division, and they

Jimmy Gallacher takes a session. Gallacher, the trainer, often looked after David Reynolds when his dad ended up in hospital rather than on the team bus home (Southern Newspapers)

took just 9 points out of the last 28, finishing eighth, 14 points away from the promotion slot that had once seemed possible. Ron missed out on much of that run-in with a couple of minor injuries, but that was as nothing when compared to the disappointment that was around the corner.

Before the 1961/62 season got under way, football had to come to terms with the effects of the abolition of the maximum wage. Right from the outset, the new freedom of wages fractured team spirit and unity within the clubs. It set player against player, as Reynolds admitted: 'The only time I ever had words with Ted Bates was when the maximum wage was lifted. I believe I'm right in saying the increase we were offered was one pound, to twenty-one pounds. It could have been twenty-two, but certainly no more. Not quite Johnny Haynes, the first hundred-pound-a-week player, was it? Had it been across the board, perhaps it might have been accepted, but of course Terry Paine couldn't help bragging about the money he was on. We knew they'd given him forty-five pounds.

'Now, every away game we played, we were playing with ten men: Terry Paine just stood on the wing and did nothing. At home he used to turn it on, but away we played for him and he stood about. So, while we appreciated Terry's ability, we weren't happy.

Just before the first game of the season, against Plymouth at home, all of the first-team players said, "Unless we get some satisfaction, you haven't got a team for Saturday!" About an hour and a half before the game started, Ted relented and we were all put on twenty-five pounds. Then, just about five minutes before half-time, I went for a high ball, came down awkwardly, and fractured my right ankle.'

Nowadays, we're used to fractures routinely healing in a couple of months, but back in 1961, that was usually season-long damage, and so it proved for Ron. His season lasted just forty minutes. It was a frustrating spell as he saw the Saints improve to sixth, but again just fail to make that extra push required to win promotion to Division One, missing out by nine points.

It was a doubly upsetting time because the Reynolds family had just moved down to the local area from their Haslemere home, as son David recalls: 'The move to Southampton was a shock for us: none of the family wanted to move. I was nearly a teenager, my younger brother was 8, and my baby sister 2. But Dad saw it as a new lease of life: the Saints had given him a chance to use his experience as an established first-choice keeper. When he was at Spurs he did a lot of coaching at private schools – Harrow, Winchester, places like that – and that took up his spare time, so we didn't see a lot of him as a result. He didn't earn a great deal of money, but he built up contacts and also learned about coaching, and was able to recommend youngsters to clubs. The scouting systems weren't very sophisticated then, it was pot luck, I think, but he was in a good position to pass on names.

'But when he went to Southampton, he had to curtail some of the FA coaching because of the travelling. He was also thinking that coaching wouldn't pay the bills once he packed in football, so he started looking for other things. He was friendly with Bill Tinworth, who had a tailor's shop, and they went into partnership to open a shop in Havant, near Portsmouth. Mum and Dad then decided we'd move down there, to Langston Harbour. That was typical of Dad, thinking about the future. In those days there were very few players who thought: Well, I'd better get a second career going. They were footballers, and that was it.

'Langston Harbour was a nice place, yet somewhat remote, and the culture shock for me, my brother and sister was pretty terrible. Likewise, it was difficult for my mother, having to settle in an alien county, left at home each day with just the baby for company – it wasn't easy for her to make new friends. I was twelve, had done a year at senior school, and found it very difficult to adjust. It was a much tougher regime down there, a bit of an eye-opener for me, but I used to go down to Fratton Park, ironically enough, for football training, so I enjoyed that. I got plenty of good-humoured stick because my dad played for Southampton. I enjoyed watching Southampton because they were on a bit of a roll at the time. They had some good players: Terry Paine, Ron Davies and players who came up through the ranks – and later Martin Chivers, Mick Channon and Bobby Stokes.'

By the time Ron was back in harness for 1962/63, Southampton had rung the changes, with Stuart Williams, the Welsh international full-back, and David Burnside joining from West Bromwich Albion and the forward George Kirby coming in from Plymouth. Ron missed the first four games, but was soon back between the sticks for what was a monumental season in the club's history. A tremendous cup run combined with an awful winter to create a fixture pile-up which has rarely been equalled, before or since.

There was no question that Ted Bates was building a side that was assured of success in the upper reaches of Division Two, but, as Ron suggested, that wasn't enough: 'Ted had his eyes on promotion all the time. I think he felt that if clubs like Ipswich and Leyton Orient could go up, so could Southampton, and of course he was right. We didn't have vast amounts of money to spend, but we used what we had wisely and we slowly gathered momentum. Although, in that 1962/63 season, we had a dreadful start and were bottom early on.

The 1962–63 line-up (Southern Newspapers)

But Ted kept faith with what he was doing and we were out of trouble by Christmas.'

Then the weather closed in. Between Boxing Day and 1 March the Saints played just three games, two of which were in the FA Cup. Once the season started to roll again in March, they had eighteen league games left, almost half a season's worth. And they were still in the cup, moving on to the sixth round by beating Sheffield United, 1–0. That saw them play Nottingham Forest three times in an attempt to get a result. The second replay took place on neutral ground, with Ron returning to White Hart Lane and celebrating with a clean sheet as Forest were put to the sword, 5–0. It was naturally a night Ron remembered well: 'They were good games against Forest: a 1–1 and a 3–3, before the White Hart Lane match. It was lovely to go back to Tottenham to play for the first time since I'd left, and, like any professional, especially when you've been, if not exactly rejected, at least dropped out of the pecking order. It's nice to return and show them what they're missing. As it happened, I didn't have much to do because we completely dominated the game from start to finish. That set us up for a semi-final against Manchester United.'

As is often the case, having a semi-final on the horizon caused Southampton's league form to take a dip, and they took just one point from games at Norwich and home and away against Plymouth, although they did win at Walsall, who would be relegated at the end of the season. It was a perfectly understandable reaction, with the Saints nowhere near promotion and free of any real fears of relegation. They prepared for the Villa Park showdown by thumping Swansea 3–0 just five days before the meeting with the side Busby was still rebuilding after Munich. Bobby Charlton and Bill Foulkes had by now been joined by the mercurial Denis Law, the vision and intelligence of Johnny Giles and the exuberance of Paddy Crerand. Ron vividly remembered the build-up to the match: 'Like all lower-division sides, you go into those games to enjoy them and without any real pressure; though, of course, you accept that the odds are definitely against you. That gives you a certain freedom, and in those

Denis Law put the Saints out of the Cup at Villa Park (Sport & General)

Night match at The Dell

days, even against a side as great as Manchester United, you always felt that the teams from lower down had a chance. A mid-table First Division side now would have very little chance against a team like Manchester United, but then the disparity wasn't so great.

'Having said that, of course, the ability that United had in that team was frightening, which was a great credit to Matt Busby. He had simply got on with the job of rebuilding the club for a second time after the Munich disaster, just as he had rebuilt it when he went there after the war. Perhaps they didn't achieve all they could have, but that was because there were a lot of very good English teams around at that time. Liverpool were coming strong with Shankly, Revie transformed Leeds, Spurs were still a force, Everton were powerful, then Arsenal came good. The competition was very stiff then, but if you wanted to see great football, Old Trafford was always the first place you would go.

'Funnily enough, the game against United wasn't a classic. For them, it was the chance to win a trophy for the first time since Munich, so it mattered a great deal, and that inhibited them. They weren't the usual Manchester United. We were grateful for that, but we'd run out of steam and I think we let the occasion get to us. We'd played fifteen games in eight weeks, a lot of them big FA Cup games, and the three matches with Forest had taken a lot out of us. Denis Law scrambled a goal and we couldn't get level. It was a great shame: we would have loved to have gone to Wembley, but it wasn't to be.'

Southampton proved what a strong team spirit they had by regrouping well and performing creditably in the eight games they still had to play in May. They took 11 of the 16 points on offer to finish with 42, leaving them in solid mid-table and with some reasons for optimism for the following season, particularly with young Martin Chivers ready to take his place in the Saints' attack.

But for Ron Reynolds, not yet thirty-five, that day out at Villa Park in front of 68,312 spectators was to be a last hurrah. Injury, the constant enemy throughout his playing career, was about to have the final say.

Ron's retirement in the press

CHAPTER SEVENTEEN

Ron's last appearance in the match-day programme,
away to Portsmouth, 28th September 1963

The 1963/64 season was a mere ten games old when Ron Reynolds suffered what was becoming the obligatory early-season injury, at Fratton Park. Son David was in the crowd: 'Dad took me and a friend and I remember it so well. Pompey attacked and Southampton cleared it, but for some reason I looked back and I saw the old man was really struggling and his shoulder was just ripped right out, you could see it sagging halfway down where his arm should be. It was horrible, horrible. He got carted off to hospital, and I think it was the trainer, Jimmy Gallacher who picked me and my mates up and took us down to the local hospital to see him, and then drove us and Dad home.

Reynolds shines as 'stars' flop

REYNOLDS

From BOB PENNINGTON: Holland 2 Football Combination 0

AMSTERDAM, Wednesday.—"Forgotten" goalkeeper Ron Reynolds, discarded by Spurs into the Third Division with Southampton, came back to glory here tonight and saved our shattered Soccer pride from utter humiliation before 40,000 contemptuous Dutchmen.

Thirty - one - year - old Reynolds, shielding his contact lenses from the harsh glare of the floodlights at this Olympic Stadium, made nearly a dozen great saves in the grand manner that once brought him England "B" honours.

"At Tottenham I got one game a fortnight and believe I was forgotten," Reynolds told me as he walked off to a roar of cheers. "Now at Southampton I feel I belong in this game again."

But this was a bitter 21st-birthday lesson for Southampton's right-winger Terry Paine.

THE LESSON

Last week boy Paine looked a star of tomorrow with his display for Young England against the Dutch at Sheffield.

Tonight, in this select British company with a total transfer value of well over £160,000, Paine learned the harsh truth that even the Dutch have now passed us in basic Soccer skills—and tactics.

This was the Football Combination's first defeat in Holland.

Thirty-four-year-old international veteran inside-left Kees Rijvers, the match master, split the British defence in the 11th minute for inside-right Henek Groot to chip the ball over Reynolds's head for the first goal.

THE TRAGEDY

The 65th minute was mixed in triumph and tragedy for Reynolds.

The crowd rose to his fantastic save from Rijvers. But from the corner kick Reynolds leaped to touch Groot's header, only to slip and see the ball trickle behind him over the line.

Phil Woosnam, only forward to rival the Dutch in artistry, gave Ron Tindall a "gift" chance which was blazed over the bar, and in the end it was Reynolds. Reynolds, Reynolds—glory be.

FOOTBALL COMBINATION.— Reynolds (Southampton); Bond (West Ham); Cantwell (West Ham); Anderton (Chelsea); Norman (Spurs); Appleton (Leicester); Paine (Southampton); Woosnam (West Ham); Tindall (Chelsea); Dunmore (West Ham); Sydenham (Southampton).

'He was pretty groggy, he had a really bad dislocation. He'd injured his collarbone as well, and that was it, he didn't play again after that. It never healed properly – in those days, the treatment you got wasn't very good, it wasn't scientific. It was in the early days of ultrasound, it was all pretty Heath Robinson, so the repairs they did to injuries were nothing like what you'd expect now. The injury finished his golf as well, his shoulder was so distorted he couldn't swing a club – if you saw him swimming, it was like watching a hump backed whale!"

Reflecting on his final injury, Ron said, 'I think I knew straight away that this was going to be a really bad one, because it was obvious the shoulder was very badly dislocated: it was just detached. And there was a bad injury to the collar bone too. When you get to thirty-five, with any bad injury you think: Am I going to play again? I hoped I'd get over it, because I thought I would be able to play for another four or five seasons after that one, but the damage to the shoulder, the socket, everything, made it impossible. I was very sad about it, but you have to get on with life.'

Given his coaching background, that might have been an avenue for Ron to pursue. Indeed, during his rehabilitation, he did a lot of coaching work, at Winchester, Eton, Highgate, Charterhouse, Witley, Lanesborough and even coaching the Gurkhas. (This brought in £39 7s 6d (£39.37) plus expenses, but after other costs, Ron's meticulous records showed that coaching had actually delivered a net loss on the year of £2 18s 2d (£2.91). At least this was mitigated by his share of the Players' Pool generated by the FA Cup run to the semi-final. Ron collected £23 in total, some way short of the thousands that today's players would rake in, but still a nice little addition to his basic earnings of £1658 with Southampton.)

But if coaching was a non-profit making business, what about management? With his contacts, surely there was a chance for him to move into the managerial chair somewhere? If there had been, it wasn't a prospect that appealed, because like his great Tottenham friend, Danny Blanchflower, the whole idea turned his stomach. Such coaching experience would seem to indicate that the obvious next step would be management, but on that score Ron concurred with his friend Danny Blanchflower (or at least what Danny *claimed* was his opinion): 'Danny always told me that he would never take up managing. He said, "I would have to be doing things or considering things that I would hate as a player now if my manager did it to me. I could never do it to the players." So imagine my surprise when he took on the Chelsea job. I suppose he just felt he couldn't do without football. But I was very much in agreement with him over his distaste for management.'

Nevertheless, Ron's friend Brian Pearce believes that he could have stayed in the game and been very successful: 'I thought he was a very good coach. He had the ability and the enthusiasm to put things over, and he put me in mind of another coach from that time, Bobby Robson. The way they could talk about the game enthused those around them; they had great drive and got complete attention from the boys . . . However, you can be the best coach in the world, but if the manager gets the sack, his staff go with him, so I think he felt that, with three children to look after, it was too precarious a profession. And they were very settled where they were back in Haslemere and I think the fact that coaching does mean you have to move around the country didn't really appeal greatly either. So I think he turned to the financial services as a more secure and settled option.'

So it was that Ron severed his full-time ties with football and instead threw himself into what he saw as his post-football career, working in the tailor's business he had helped set up in Havant. But, as David Reynolds recalls, the transition to life in the 'real world' was not the smoothest: 'When he finished, the tailor's business didn't get

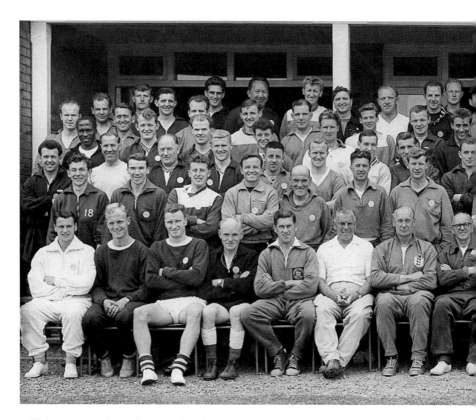

off the ground, so they packed it in and we came back to Haslemere after being down there for a year. They'd set up a shop in a new arcade in Havant, but it was on the edge of a huge council estate and it just never got going. That put him back financially for quite a while. It was a very difficult time for him, because, having made some kind of provision for after he retired, it all fell away pretty quickly and he was left having to think of something else that he could do.

'He was in touch with a financial services firm, Clifford & Geoffrey, in Croydon, whom he started working with part time. He seemed to enjoy it and effectively retrained to work in that field. Not the sort of thing that David Seaman will have to do when he packs up, I shouldn't think!

'Dad always had a head for figures, and it suited his character: he was always very meticulous, methodical, efficient – too much so sometimes. He loved gardening, but it all had to be just right: he'd be

Awardees of the Preliminary Staff Coaching Certificate, Lilleshall, June 1961. Ron is fifth from left on the front row. Bobby Robson, Don Howe, and Jock Wallace are far left, front row (Arden Studios)

out there cutting the grass with nail scissors. So he had the mentality for it and he did OK there. It meant that he didn't take a big drop in salary after Southampton. He was there for a couple of years before he left with another bloke, and they set up their own partnership in 1967, which was a big decision.

'If you've been in football, to start a whole new life from scratch is very tough. But he worked hard, door knocking, cold calling, out all hours, and it was down to him that it worked. But a lot of football connections came good for him. David Chadwick, whom he knew from Southampton, became a sub-agent of sorts; Willie Maddren at Middlesbrough helped with contacts up north; and Tony Knapp at Southampton was a good ambassador as well, spreading the gospel.

I was training in accountancy then, so I did a bit of financial work for them, and after about a couple of years Dad decided to dissolve the partnership and asked me if I wanted to come in with him, which I did. That went from 1970 to 1987.

'It was never easy, but then I don't think it's ever easy being in business with your family, especially when we used to clash a lot, because we had different temperaments and different outlooks on life and business. He was very outspoken about everything: he could argue about anything. He always had an answer, he'd rarely admit to being wrong and in business we had many disputes because he'd get a bee in his bonnet about something. Nevertheless, we were both pulling in the same direction. It was as important for me as it was for Dad, as I had a family too after I got married in 1972, so we both wanted it to succeed.

'When we were struggling to get it going, I was working all hours, and I eventually decided we were driving ourselves into the ground and that quality of life for the family was far more important. But he wouldn't have it: the business was more important, because if you couldn't make it work, you weren't looking after your family. I can see his point of view, but I don't necessarily agree with it.

'I'm a trained accountant, concerned with the cash-flow side of things, making sure we were generating profits, while Dad was more from the old school, I suppose. He was much more concerned with the idea of the firm building a reputation, making sure that people were looked after, even if he made no money out of it. He was a great one for chasing lost causes. If somebody was wronged he'd pursue it, if only to get the satisfaction of winning. I used to think that was all very laudable, but it wasn't making any money for us. That carried on for seventeen years.'

For all the personal clashes that were part and parcel of business – and family – life, for David, the years that the two spent working together were ultimately cathartic and enabled him to step out from his father's shadow and become his own man: 'When I was young, it was automatic for me to follow in his footsteps and be a goalkeeper. But, especially when you're younger, it's very difficult when you're always introduced as "the son of" rather than in your own right. I wasn't too conscious of it until we went into business, when I became a bit cheesed off. I felt I had to make a name for myself in business. I knew I wouldn't make it in football because I didn't have the temperament for it. Looking back, possibly being known as Ron Reynolds' son was one of the reasons for that, and that's why I admire the very few pros who are sons of big names, because most won't make it. You're always in the shadows. So business was perhaps my opportunity, because I had more experience than Dad in that environment, and I could show him and the world that I could be successful. To his credit, Dad came round, and he worked his socks off alongside me to build up the business. He started it, but I finished it – in the end I was doing the negotiating, and that was the making of me.'

Hard though Ron worked, there would always be some time for football, especially in the early days of his retirement, when he did a great deal of scouting work, not only for Southampton, but for Crystal Palace, as David remembers: 'He liked watching the game, and the scouting for Crystal Palace kept him in touch. He was very friendly with Bert Head there, though he wasn't keen on Malcolm Allison when he took over, which I suppose wasn't surprising: they came from different worlds. He did a bit for Southampton, too: Mick Channon was one he found, and Bobby Stokes, and he enjoyed going on scouting missions all over the place. It meant he was out on the parks, and he liked that – he used to watch me sometimes, and especially my son later on. He much preferred boys' football to the senior game. When we did go, he was highly critical of that.'

Ron certainly was no lover of the modern game, as he stated towards the end of his life: 'I watched a Leeds game up at Spurs and at the end of it I said, "Arthur Rowe would have turned in his grave if he'd seen that!" We've gone back to the game where it's hit the ball up the middle and hope for the best. I think it's been brought about by this blessed ruling about passes back to the goalkeepers. It encourages goalkeepers, if they've got time, to look up, push it a little further, look up, push it a little further and when they do hit it, it's invariably down the middle and the defence has had time to regroup, if there's any regrouping necessary. It was a case that the Leeds defence – all tall lads, apart from the left-back – had to do was head it out. If I'd been a Tottenham forward, I'd have gone in at half-time and said to the manager, "For Christ's sake, let's get playing football!"

'At Tottenham, there's a club called the Legends. For about four seasons I've taken advantage of it: you go up, have a nice meal and talk to all the old mates – Tommy Harmer, Les Bennett, Ronnie Burgess. But you look around you and it's gone crazy. They couldn't care less now about the genuine supporter. It's all about getting the money in from various banks and large firms and it annoys me very much. I do a hundred-and-forty-mile round trip to see a bloody lousy game in which the players are earning – not *earning*, but *receiving* – fantastic remuneration and it's crazy.'

Not every encounter with old colleagues was as happy as those Ron enjoyed at the Legends, though. He remembered one chance meeting with Sir Alf Ramsey in particular: 'I drove up for an England game at Wembley, parked the car in a side lane and walked about a mile through a rough area. I had relatives with me and we were joking, saying, "When we get back tonight the car won't be there." As we walked in I saw Alf coming away from the ground. By this time, of course, he was nothing to do with England. As we walked towards each other I said, "Alf, how are you getting on?" He looked at me and said, "It's Ron isn't it?" I said, "Yes," and with that he said, "Well, I can't stop." And off he went! That was the first occasion I'd seen Alf since he'd tried to get me to sign for Ipswich all those years before. Five minutes wouldn't have made any difference to him whatsoever. But he was a loner, there's no doubt about that.'

Incidents such as that can only have exacerbated a disenchantment with the game which Ron's son David remembers vividly: 'I think he became very disillusioned with football, as it "progressed". In the 1960s and 1970s, he didn't like a lot of the things that went on. I went to that dire Chelsea–Aston Villa FA Cup Final a couple of years back, the year after Dad died, and I thought of him then, because he wouldn't have enjoyed that. We'd watch football on telly and argue about something or other. I don't think he was jealous of the money they earned. It was more that he felt there were too many prima donnas, that they weren't appreciative of how easy they have it compared with the old days. It was a harsh regime, the future was uncertain, conditions were poor, equipment was awful. All that has completely changed and I think he felt that players now take it for granted. It was literally a different ball game then: the ball itself, the kit was antiquated, there was no scientific basis to any of the stuff. Nobody ever thought about redesigning goalkeeper's gloves: they were like old string gloves. Dad also had an old goalkeeper's jumper which he wore in the garden. It was made out of very itchy wool. I can remember trying it on when I was a nipper, thinking: Oh! I couldn't wear this.

'I don't know what he would make of the gloves and the equipment now. I still play sometimes and the huge gloves are a great advantage. Your hands aren't cold or wet, there's an extra inch on your fingers, it's easier to hold, punch or parry and they really protect your hands. The worst thing for goalkeepers was they were always dislocating fingers or thumbs. The leather ball was much heavier, and, with the square posts they used to have instead of the round ones you have now, you could easily trap your fingers against them or underneath them. You never strapped them up, you just clicked them back in, put your string gloves back on and off you went. The trainer would come on, you'd look away, clench your teeth, it hurt like mad when he pushed it back, but once he'd done that, you carried on. Dad did take a battering, there's no doubt about it.

'Even if he wasn't always a fan of the football, he still liked going to the games. He loved the feel of the place, and I suppose it's like the smell of the greasepaint. You get addicted to that big-match atmosphere. My loyalty is to Southampton – I was old enough to take it in when he was there, and they were becoming increasingly successful, and Dad had a big part in that: he brought stability to the back line with his experience. They thought a lot of him and everyone was very sad when he had to pack up. So I always preferred to go to The Dell. But if *he* had a choice, he'd go to Spurs, when the Legends Club was up and running after Terry Venables started it. It was free to start with, but then Alan Sugar started cutting back and they had to pay for it, and he wasn't impressed with that! But he liked meeting up with the old guys he hadn't seen in donkey's years, though I don't know that he made many lifelong friends in football. He was isolated in Haslemere; he'd come back here after training and wouldn't see his team-mates until the next training session, whereas the others might all go out and play golf or something because they lived near the club.

'He had a bit of heart trouble, and in 1987 decided to retire, do a bit of consultancy, so we sold the business on to our accountants and I stayed on as managing director. After he retired, he mellowed a lot. Losing the pressure of running a business did that, as did the heart-attack – he realised he couldn't get so stressed about things. It's just such a shame that somebody who avoided the extremes of life, was clean living, looked after himself, very fit, could then just keel over and die on his seventy-first birthday. Right to the end, though, he was still argumentative. I just gave up sometimes, because you knew you weren't going to win. If he were ever with his eldest sister, I used to walk out: it was futile even to bother with them. But that was Dad: very righteous, very difficult to prove wrong. That's perhaps why he made so many enemies. But if you think you're right, what's wrong with having principles?'

From start to finish, Ron Reynolds was his own man, often on the fringes, both professionally and personally, but that distance gave him an original perspective on many issues, and provided him with the emotional balance to take the punches that life in football threw at him, as his son David says: 'Being a goalkeeper, you have to have something loose somewhere! If you have a high as a keeper, it's like scoring a goal. I don't think full-backs or midfielders can get the same feeling out of a good tackle and the same sense of satisfaction at the end of a game. If you've saved a penalty or made two or three blinding saves, everybody wants to be your friend and you feel ten feet tall. But, the other way, one blunder turns the game and that's it. There can't be any other position where you are so pilloried and you can never forget it, people won't let you. You're always remembered for dropping the ball instead of the ninety-nine times out of a

Ron and Betty celebrate fifty years of marriage in 1998

hundred where you've caught it or punched it or parried it away.

'Very few footballers can make it on the back of talent and hard work alone. There's a big slice of pot luck in there. In whatever era, it's being in the right place at the right time, doing the right thing and being spotted by the right people from the right club. It's such a combination of factors, and then you can get there and break your leg. It's a gamble.

'When you're winning, they all want to know you. When you're losing, nobody wants to know, and Dad always understood that. Football is all about success. On that level, because he never quite established himself at the very top of the game, I suppose in the end his life never brought total fulfilment, but whose does?'

Perhaps it didn't bring fulfilment in the sense of a cupboard full of medals. But it was a principled life, a life lived according to his own morality, which never cracked, even under the most severe provocation. So maybe Ron's life didn't bring total fulfilment. But it was a life well lived and a life worth living. Is there a better epitaph?

INDEX

Compiled by
INDEXING SPECIALISTS (UK),
202 Church Road, Hove, East Sussex
BN3 2DJ. Tel: 01273 738299.
email: richardr@indexing.co.uk
Website: www.indexing.co.uk